Confessions of a Berlitz-Tape Chicana

CHICANA & CHICANO VISIONS OF THE AMÉRICAS

CHICANA & CHICANO VISIONS OF THE AMÉRICAS

Confessions of a
Berlitz-Tape Chicana

Demetria Martínez

UNIVERSITY OF OKLAHOMA PRESS : NORMAN

ALSO BY DEMETRIA MARTÍNEZ

Mother Tongue (Tempe, Ariz., 1994; New York, 1996)
Breathing between the Lines: Poems (Tucson, Ariz., 1997)
The Devil's Workshop (Tucson, Ariz., 2002)

Library of Congress Cataloging-in-Publication Data

Martínez, Demetria, 1960–
    Confessions of a Berlitz-tape Chicana / Demetria Martínez
    p. cm.— (Chicana & Chicano visions of the Américas ; v. 4)
    ISBN 0–8061–3706–1 (alk. paper)—ISBN 0–8061–3722–3 (pbk. : alk. paper)
    1. Martínez, Demetria, 1960– 2. Authors, American—20th century—
Biography. 3. Catholic women—United States—Biography. 4. Mexican
American authors—Biography. 5. Mexican American women—Biography.
6. Bilingualism—United States. I. Title. II. Series.

PS3563.A7333337Z469 2005
818'.5409—dc22
[B]
                                                                2005041775

Confessions of a Berlitz-Tape Chicana is Volume 4 in
the Chicana & Chicano Visions of the Américas series.

For my niece and nephews:
Rachel Dolores, Benjamin Theodore, and David Demetrio

No de piedra, ni madera
De mármol ni de cemento
Un monumento de letras
Nacido del pensamiento.

Not of stone, nor wood
Marble nor cement
A monument of letters
Born of thought.

Luis Martínez, "Un Monumento"

Contents

Columnas Catolicas: Hola, Mary

Columnas Fronteras: Inherit the Earth

Columnas en Tiempos de Guerra: Hell No

Acknowledgments

I wish to thank the following publications, where most of the essays in *Confessions of a Berlitz-Tape Chicana* first appeared, some in an edited version:

National Catholic Reporter
World Literature Today
Progressive Magazine
Arizona Republic
Sojourners Magazine

The radio program *Latino USA* first aired the commentary "Inherit the Earth."

And mil gracias to my editors at the *National Catholic Reporter*; my colleagues at the William Joiner Center for the Study of War and Social Consequences at the University of Massachusetts, Boston; my agent, Ellen Levine; and Robert Con Davis-Undiano, who suggested I undertake this project. Bless you Norty and Summers Kalishman and Norma Gutierrez, who offered keys to houses and a bed when troubled spirits besieged my own house.

.

Confessions of a Berlitz-Tape Chicana

Introduction

A long time ago I learned that if I were to stay sane, I had to jot down notes in the margins of the official story, the story as handed down in everything from church catechisms that are less than kind to women to proclamations of war that are making Earth a very unwelcoming place for all life forms. The margins are a great place to debunk. To tell your own version of the story. To imagine what a better world might look like. To rest up. Soon enough you'll feel a tickle in your gut. That's not fear. It's desire to act, go forth and bless this mess, create a world worthy of being inherited by the poor, in which the rich are sent away empty.

Of course I brought to the margins a certain sensibility: I'm a Chicana, a Catholic, the spiritual descendant of Sor Juana Inés de la Cruz and César Chávez, Santa Teresa de Ávila and Archbishop Oscar Romero, Dolores Huerta and Juan Diego, to whom Guadalupe appeared speaking Nahuatl. Like so many of my generation, I passionately yearn to pray and yet also to act. To divine what alchemical interaction of the two might grant us the wisdom we need, especially in the wake of the 9/11 tragedy and the U.S. invasion of Iraq under false pretenses. Hatred and the threat of mutual destruction binds this world together as never before, yet so, too, do mass communications and images of spirit that we share across cultures. Our traditional altars have evolved to include the Dalai Lama, Mary, Jesus, Buddha, Saraswati, and more. All insist that we never give up hope.

Oh yes, I am a believer. But I also live with the knowledge that nobody has ever produced a photograph of God, so I am condemned to write from the edges of belief, often teetering into nonbelief, but there is much to be learned, everything to be learned, in the murky nights of the soul. This is when I turn to La Llorona, the wailing woman of Chicano mythology, who wanders the banks of the river, crying out for her dead children. There's no resurrecting the innocents we are acutely conscious of losing to violence early in the twenty-first century. La Llorona cries out, "hay, mis hijos!" And I record her stark lamentation in the margins of official press releases about smart bombs and in the margins of banned photographs of coffins at Dover Air Force Base. "What God?" I add to my notations.

But then . . . beauty breaks through. A young man working to stop the genocide in Sudan comes to me with a petition as lovely as any poem and asks for a signature. My niece declares that death is like "borning," except in the opposite direction. Look, there's our Lady of Guadalupe in a Zapatista ski mask, hovering above millions of people marching in New York City against the war in Iraq! Time again to hope in a God who dwells not in heaven but in such moments and people here on earth.

Over many years the notes I put down in the margins added up. I arranged them into columns and other pieces, some simple, some elaborate, all deeply personal: pillars rising into the New Mexico skies, the architecture of my place and faith. I'm no writer of manifestos; I'm a storyteller. As such, my job is to aid and abet, inspire and incite, refresh and console. I hope that you, the reader, will join me in an exchange. If something snags at your spirit, grab a pencil, go to the margins, and put down your own thoughts. We're in this plot together, no matter how different our backgrounds and beliefs. Our stories entwine like trumpet vines. Together may we break the spell of the official story and grant ourselves and the gods the open-ended destiny that is our right. ▪

2004

Columnas Privadas

Birth Day

Invocation

(Dream: Boston, 2001)

I am searching for just the right cemetery, a proper burial ground for my ancestors' ashes. I have with me small containers, urns perhaps, that hold their remains. A grassy field stretches out before me. The proprietors suggest I consider small trellises that they sell for use as markers. Vines can be planted at each site. I like the idea of the trellises, but something nags at me. Beautiful as the cemetery is, I sense that it is too far away from the Southwest.

Scene change: I am savoring a cup of coffee—or is it Mexican chocolate—sipping slowly from a mug I hold in both hands. There are grains at the bottom. These I stir with a spoon before lifting the mug again to my lips. Somehow I know that the grains are my ancestors' ashes. I feel peaceful and strong; this is as it should be. Their spirits are safe with me.

Salvador Jaramillo and Teresa Trujillo, Joaquín Tafoya and Guadalupe Torres, Francisco Antonio Chaves and Gregoria Padilla, José Gabriel Sanches and Manuela Padilla, José Gabaldón and María Gertrudis Chaves, Antonio García and María Josefa Martín . . . these are the names of just a smattering of my grandfather's people, born in the 1700s, many of them married at the church in Tomé, New Mexico, south of Albuquerque.

Then there are my grandmother's people, those born in the 1600s: José Telles Jirón and Catalina Romero, Andrés Hurtado and Bernadina de Salas y Trujillo, Diego Montoya and María de Vera, Miguel Vásquez de Lara and Juana de Alcalá, Ignacio de Aragón and Sebastiana Ortiz, Matías Romero and Ángela Vallejo, Miguel de Castro Xabalera and Juana Guerrero. The son of the Laras was born in Villa de los Lagos, Asturias, Spain. The birthplace of the daughter of the Castros was Sombrerete, Zacatecas, Mexico. Then there is _____ Carvajal, first name unknown, married to Fernando D. y Chávez. According to church citations in Fray Angélico Chávez's *New Mexico Families,* _____ Carvajal's mother's name was Isabel Holguín. Isabel, the citation notes, was accused by church officials in 1626 of trafficking in "magic roots."

These are only a few of the names that fill the genealogy charts from my mother's side of the family. These names have moved with me from city to city, forever filed and refiled. With each packing and unpacking of my belongings, guilt has dogged me. I should be doing research, I think, uncovering everything possible about my antepasados, setting the record straight, whatever the record might be.

The stories sprawl all over the place: the ancestor who was part of Juan de Oñate's party, which oversaw the brutal torture and murder of Acoma Pueblo Indians; the "full-blooded" Isleta Pueblo ancestor, Josefa de Hinojos; the Navajo great-great-grandmother, who exposed my grandpa Luis to enough of her language that he could help Navajo people at the courthouse in Albuquerque, where he worked as an interpreter; the "conversos," who practiced a mishmash of Jewish and Catholic rituals, mixing Ladino in with their Spanish. In other words, these were a mestizo people, creating themselves anew every generation in an unrelenting odyssey away from the Spanish ideal of "limpia sangre," or pure blood.

It appears that at least in this lifetime, my ancestors will not be my particular research project. Years ago I copied the genealogy charts and sent them to my mothers' siblings. Maybe one day a second or third or fourth cousin will use the information as a basis for a dissertation. I understand that research is not the burial ground I am looking for, though I know that the act of research could produce amazing flowering vines, rooted in the humus of the past.

The way I pay my dues to the past is with ritual. I begin with this written meditation: the naming of names and remembrance of the dream in which I welcomed the ashes into the temple of my body. In my blood runs everything from the most murderous impulses of those who preceded me, to the best strivings and sweetest hopes.

Which raises the questions. How does one live so as to atone, to bring full circle? How to draw strength from the knowledge that the antepasados are here and now? How to finish the sentence that was their lives and write myself into the odyssey that is my own future, my own sentence, in that never-ending work in progress known as the New World? ■

2002

Lines in the Sand

Ever since the Spanish and the Indians mixed over five hundred years ago, makeup has gone orange on Chicana complexions. Throughout my teens, twenties, and much of my thirties, I would emerge from drugstores, my wrists slashed with lipstick samples, my cheeks primed with blush, my jawline finished with foundation. Cover Girl, Maybelline, Revlon: I have graced cosmetic companies with more of my consumer dollars than I dare admit.

But those mirrors at the counters that glare like headlights? Take my word for it. They are part of a vast capitalist conspiracy against women with olive skin.

As any Chicana will tell you, the one mirror that never lies is your rearview mirror at high noon. The traffic light turns red. You peer through dangling rosary beads, hope springing eternal. You just bought enough makeup to touch up a Diego Rivera mural; you asked not for high art, merely good coverage.

But it is not to be. In the time it took to drive ten blocks from Walgreens, your blush, lipstick, and foundation have taken on a sorrowful orange flush. The guy behind you honks; God only knows when the light turned green. The only reason to hold your head up for the rest of the drive is your eye shadow, its colors fixed as beautifully as those in a Navajo sand painting.

So what exactly is olive skin?

My father is café con very little leche. Mom is peaches and cream. Why my coloring evokes the small ovoid fruit of a Mediterranean evergreen tree confounds me. For years curiosity has lured me into gourmet delis and international markets, where

I have scrutinized jars of olives and bottles of virgin pressed oils looking for similarities to my own skin color. Nada.

I turn to the *American Heritage Dictionary*. The color olive, it says, is "A yellow green of low to medium lightness and low to moderate saturation." Huh?

"I can't keep on throwing away money on makeup at Walgreens," I confess to Charlotte, an African American who works in cosmetics at JCPenney.

Charlotte is examining my face like a surgeon about to lower the scalpel. "You've got a ton of yellow," she says. "A lot of my Hispanic ladies buy the wrong makeup because they don't think of themselves as on the yellow side. They think it's more of an Asian thing." She swirls a cotton pad in a powder compact labeled "Sand."

"Try this. Take the mirror outdoors and stand in the sun," she instructs. "Remember, you want to match your skin, not lighten it or darken it."

I forge ahead with the experiment in the blazing sun. Sand it is. Now this is a *real* discovery. Five hundred years after the conquest, this Chicana stumbles upon the perfect face powder, part of a line of makeup made for women of color by a supermodel who hails from Africa.

Call it cosmetic justice. The Spaniards were enamored of the concept of sangre limpia, yet their veins were saturated with the blood of Moors and Jews, African slaves and the indigenous peoples of the New World. Is it any wonder that daughters and sons of la raza cósmica—indeed, all Latinos—subvert the color schemes imposed upon us by census and society alike?

One afternoon at a Chicago hotel, I was putting on my face in preparation for a poetry reading I was to give that night with Nikki Giovanni. Listening to National Public Radio, I was surprised to learn that the great physicist Stephen Hawking was speaking at a conference on cosmetology. I turned the volume up.

Cosmology, you idiot, I said to myself.

But I should have probed more deeply. The word "cosmetics" comes from the Greek word "kosmos," meaning order. Such etymologies can seem esoteric—until you turn forty. When my day came, I thought about the many cultures whose philosophies hold that physical beauty is a reflection of harmony, an order arising from good relations with others, nature, and the deities.

My makeup expenditures took a prodigious plunge.

Olive skin? Sisters, time to move on. Let's straighten our rearview mirrors and press on the gas pedal. Another five hundred years is just around the corner. Our little planet has an appointment for a makeover. We had better show up on time. ▪

2002

What Is to Be Done?

Permit me to introduce you to my alter ego: Her name is Louise. She writes very good obituaries for the Belen, New Mexico, newspaper. After work she goes home, catches a Spanish soap opera, writes letters, and maybe does her nails. She goes to bed early. The years float by. She opens a used bookstore. She dies peacefully of old age.

I need Louise. The fact that she is a figment of my imagination has never stopped her from reminding me that I always have the option to quit this noisy life of activism and live out a different story in a speck of a town far from the change-the-world crowd. I see her tidying up her obits. It's Friday. Her plans for tonight are to pick up a bean and cheese burrito somewhere and go home and begin yet another mystery by the British author P. D. James.

Time to pack my things and head for Belen, I think, trying to remember where I put my suitcase, but before I can take two steps a voice thunders: "From Pacifica Radio . . . THIS is *Democracy Now!*" Sure enough, four o'clock has rolled around, my radio is tuned to KUNM, and host Amy Goodman is about to deliver her daily report from her firehouse office in New York City. It's time, too, to start dinner, to brown a heaping tablespoon of flour for a pot of red chile I've got to make to go with yesterday's beans. I turn the radio up.

Lately the bad news has been matched only by the good news. In London a larger-than-life effigy of George W. Bush holding a missile was toppled in a massive demonstration. In Miami, thousands voiced their opposition to the Free Trade Area of the Americas meetings. And at the largest protest ever at Fort

Benning, Georgia, more than ten thousand demanded the closing of the notorious School of the Americas, whose graduates are trained in techniques to put down popular movements for justice in Latin America. Amy reports the straight facts—but I've come to know her voice, its major and minor notes, and I sense that she can barely contain her glee.

Back in Belen, Louise is heating up her burrito in the microwave. She bought an extra one on the off chance that I might join her. She looks up at me for a hopeful moment; then she smiles understandingly and picks up her book. I smile back wistfully. I make myself a note to call the Peace and Justice Center to double-check the time of an event I read about in the newsletter, a potluck featuring a speaker who has just returned from Iraq. The phone rings. Liz from Enlace Comunitario wants me to go over the press release for our upcoming poetry reading fundraiser for our group, an immigrant rights organization that serves Spanish-speaking victims of domestic violence. I add water to the red chile powder, savoring the aroma, watching the steam as it rises up like a prayer of thanksgiving for the communities of activism that give me a reason to carry on. ▪

2003–2004

Field of Greens

It's tax day. I should be worrying about what I reported or failed to report. Instead I'm consumed by thoughts of leafy greens as I head toward the produce department at Smith's supermarket.

Shopping used to be shopping. Now it's high-stakes gambling. Every item you place in the cart either adds years to or subtracts years from the rest of your life, depending upon which scientific study you believe.

I bag kale, collard, and mustard greens. These are smart bombs in the preemptive war against cancer. That's not all. I read recently of a man with macular degeneration who changed his diet to include "pails of kale"; within two years, he was removed from the "legally blind" list and had passed the test for a driver's license. Macular regeneration. I throw in more kale for good measure.

On now to dairy.

Nonorganic milk is said to possess everything from hormones to antibiotics and pus. I grab a gallon, subtract six months from my life, then add two because strong bones must count for something. One shelf down is the organic milk. To be sure, it tastes twice as good, yet it costs twice as much. But look! A Smith's special: Forty cents off each half gallon.

We must all do our part to support farmers who produce the stuff, I think, charity getting the better of me. I put the other milk back and stack three organics in the cart, one for this week and two to freeze. Come to think of it, we must all do our part to support the poor maligned French. I add Brie to the pile, checking to make sure it was indeed produced in France.

Next stop, liquor.

I love my Merlot. It's my afternoon delight, with olives, cheese, and the *Frida* soundtrack. This ritual (I don't know if the soundtrack counts) greatly lowers my risk of a heart attack. One glass of red, and my stress ebbs away, so much so that I forget that, according to other studies, I have just raised my risk of breast cancer.

Remembering this, I set the Chilean Merlot in the cart, then circle back, quickly, to produce. Here I stuff plastic bags with broccoli and cabbage to hedge my bets. Susun Weed's great book *Breast Cancer? Breast Health!* comes to mind. Eating should be a pleasure, something we do to be well, get well, stay well.

In other words, grocery shopping should not feel like preparing for a possible terrorist attack.

But it does. I'm exhausted and feeling guilty that I'm not buying organic produce at Wild Oats. Although last week I did buy supplements there. So help me God, I'll never do it again. For one thing, there are too many to choose from. People stand there for hours. The way they inspect each bottle, you'd think they were deciding on diamonds, except diamonds are cheaper. The shoppers take their pick, then look to the next aisle: blue green algae, mega B. They move one step, then another, like chess pieces. Death is the opponent.

The difference between the people who shop at Wild Oats in the northeast heights and those who shop at La Familia in the south valley is that the latter know they're going to die anyway. They grab the $6.99 "A to Zinc" and throw it in with bags of beans and rice, tomatoes, squash, sugary cereal, chiles, eggs, and tortillas. Oh yes, and pigs' feet, and a Sacred Heart holy candle. Then they move on. It's almost Cinco de Mayo. They're planning the meal to end all meals, a family picnic.

I read somewhere that a close family—garden-variety dysfunctions and all—can add years to a Latino's life. I hope so. It's fun. It's free. And besides, I like my eggs fried. ∎

2003

Oh Holy Night

Religion doesn't get any better than this: My parents and I gather round to participate in the holy sacrament of the Iowa caucuses, via television. What a night of wonders. John Kerry's and John Edwards's votes multiply like fish. Howard Dean and Richard Gephardt, by all appearances, are sent away empty. Then there's St. Dennis Kucinich, hanging in there, a sign of contradiction. Now on to New Hampshire! South Carolina! New Mexico! Dad asks me for the fiftieth time if I met the deadline for my absentee ballot. We are a family of political junkies. If you do nothing else with your life, you vote.

"I don't know about my man Wesley Clark," I tell Dad. "Kerry's looking pretty good."

"Date Clark, marry Kerry," he says, pouring himself another glass of wine. It's going to be a long evening. We want to hear the candidates' postcaucus speeches. We'll call it a night when the pundits start to repeat themselves.

Call me fickle. First I vowed to vote for Dean. My dream was of the candidate in the Lincoln Bedroom with his wife, also a physician, devising solutions to the health-care crisis until dawn. Then I switched to Clark. I imagined George Bush supporters voting for the general, if only because he looks like a white male Republican. The electability factor.

Then some sweet soul rang my doorbell and asked if I would put up a Kucinich sign. I almost caved. It's hard, if you've been raised Catholic, to turn away folks who keep the faith despite the evidence; but what would the neighbors think if I had Kucinich and Clark signs in my yard, side by side?

My commitment to Clark held steady, except when I ran into Dean supporters. Their enthusiasm, youthfulness (even if middle aged), and tendency to give everything up and follow him fueled my desire to be part of something larger than myself. I walked away from those conversations ready to sign on. Until I realized I wanted to vote for Dean's supporters, not the man himself.

"I'm voting for Kerry," I announce.

"Well, mijita, I've been waiting for returns since election night of 1948," Dad says. He reminds me that he was an errand boy for pipe-smoking politicos who gathered at the Albuquerque Hilton Hotel; glued to the radio, and calling Washington, D.C., they awaited the results of the race between Harry Truman and Thomas Dewey. Among them was Senator Dennis Chávez, the first Hispanic senator in the United States, champion of civil rights, and one of the architects of the New Deal. Dad made runs to a nearby restaurant for chicken.

"The *Chicago Daily Tribune* ran a big headline the next morning saying Dewey had won," Dad recalls with glee. "Just remember. It's not over till the fat lady sings."

Yeah, well, she sang in 2000, I think. The notes were clear: G-O-R-E. Then the Supremes stepped in and appointed Bush, who went on to invade the wrong country—no weapons of mass destruction, oops!—in the name of fighting terror. We have a long night ahead of us all right, in which we are making enemies faster than we can kill them. And it could go on for years. ∎

2004

No, I Didn't Give at the Office

Every year thousands of homeless people make the brutal pilgrimage to our city of Tucson, because street life is less lethal in a warmer climate. Everywhere, from street corners to strip malls, beggars extend empty palms. I cringe to think of the stories embedded in those lifelines: hard luck, mental illness, Vietnam. . . .

Those of us who give spare change on the streets are often chided, told that a lot of "those people" don't want to work. To be honest, that's fine by me. Our nation is full of able-bodied people who don't want to work either—they just lie about it and trudge away at jobs they hate in order to consume products they don't need. So I unload my quarters, wishing I could see Christ in the faces of the people I encounter. I rarely do. I'm too busy feeling guilty about my good luck and angry at a system that screws the poor. The hope I usually experience as an activist working for economic change goes limp.

Then I hate myself. I should save those quarters and write out more checks to United Way, or to groups that lobby Congress to repair a tattered safety net. The goal is to make charity obsolete, I tell myself.

The problem is I can't bring myself to say that out loud to someone living on the streets.

It's astonishingly narcissistic, this spin of feelings and ideological debates, given the plight of the person in front of me, who, in return, often gives me all he or she has left: a "thank-you" or "God bless you" as I walk on into the pharmacy to buy a lipstick I don't need. Such are the contradictions we live with, we who belong to that one-fifth of the world's population that controls almost 83 percent of the wealth.

I nearly veered off the road when a leftist friend said he didn't give handouts because a lot of homeless men at day's end pool their money to purchase alcohol.

Hello? What is it we of the middle class do at birthday parties, restaurants, first dates, potlucks, you name it? Except for those who have forsworn alcohol altogether, there are few among us who do not imbibe, "pooling" our money with that of friends to make for a better party, funnier jokes, and sexier one-liners.

It seems to me that whatever someone does with his or her handout is that person's business. It's one point of dignity in an otherwise hellish situation. No homeless person owes me a grant application for my generous endowment, detailing a breakdown of expenditures.

As Bishop Thomas Gumbleton said in a recent speech in Tucson, wealth belongs to God and thereby to all. That is, my money doesn't belong to me in the first place. The very jargon of charity blinds us. We imagine we are doing a favor rather than giving what is owed.

Of course, that's easier said than done. The mind races. What if the money is spent on drugs? But how can we know? And even so, who's to say the high will not lead to the crash that will lead to the rehab center or the telephone call home? (We have many runaway youths here.) Grace happens, too.

I think of all the times the Creator gave me some spare change in the form of a friendship or a beautiful day or what have you—handouts I've squandered so many times it sickens me. Yet the spare change keeps on coming with a new chance to make good.

Many cultures throughout history have held the beggar in esteem as the occasion for the sacred act of giving alms, but today in our culture the poor are blamed for being poor. You don't hear the word "beggar" here because it conjures places like Calcutta, and that dampens the giddiness of good patriots convinced we live in a prospering economy.

The homeless, be they thieves or bodhisattvas, tell the truth about our society: We'd rather throw people in the streets or in prison than exercise a modicum of political will to meet basic human needs.

Opinions differ as to the best way for individuals to spread some of the wealth, even as we work to reduce the need for charity. One of the better ideas I've heard about is a system whereby charitable groups sell vouchers worth free meals that one can give away in lieu of spare change. Such a handout might alleviate the squeamishness many feel about parting with cold cash—and more homeless might benefit.

An eternal tension: the quick fix versus the long, hard fight.

A poem by the great visionary Bertolt Brecht, called "A Bed for the Night," describes a man in New York in the depths of the Depression who appeals to passersby to get beds for the homeless:

It won't change the world
It won't improve relations among men
It will not shorten the age of exploitation
But a few men have a bed for the night
For a night the wind is kept from them
The snow meant for them falls on the roadway
Don't put down the book on reading this, man.

A few people have a bed for the night
For a night the wind is kept from them
The snow meant for them falls on the roadway
But it won't change the world
It won't improve relations among men
It will not shorten the age of exploitation. ■

1998

Call to Arms

Wary of the darkness that surrounds the path from my car to my apartment, I have built up a small arsenal of self-defense equipment: a canister of Mace on my key ring, a miniature flashlight, and a toy cell phone. These items are supposed to keep me safe.

Deployment, however, presents some real problems, particularly since I have only two arms. Consider the following scenarios, all of which I have tried.

I sometimes employ my fake cell phone as a kind of preemptive ruse. Frustrated actress that I am, I chatter into the phone (perhaps chewing gum to make it look like I am conversing), my liberated arm circling groceries like a baby on my hip. Surely a rapist would back off at the prospect of a woman hollering "call the police" into a telephone. But what if he were to call my bluff? Or, maddened with drugs, not even see my toy phone? I considered buying a real phone, but then what? Tell the guy to wait while I dial 911?

Enter the Mace. Groceries on my left hip, I grip the Mace like a gun with my right hand and walk purposefully with a shoot-to-kill (or blind-and-choke) attitude. I'm ready to spray any would-be assailant.

The danger here, of course, is posed by nature. Suppose a downwind gust pickles my eye ducts before I can run like hell? Crippling myself hardly seems like the best possible form of self-defense.

So I have that cute little flashlight I got at Home Depot to fall back on. You must understand, Tucson is dimly lit at night. Our university's astronomers, with their advanced telescopes, depend upon it.

Sometimes I combine the flashlight with one other weapon. Forget evening grocery shopping. Stepping out of my car at night, I wield flashlight and toy phone, or flashlight and Mace. Although I can't think of a way for the flashlight to backfire, the problem is that it won't do much to ward off an attacker unafraid of the light.

Obviously, I can't use the flashlight, phone, and Mace all at once. This is what I mean about not enough arms. I feel like evolution cheated women, given men's predilection for violence. The way I see it, with more arms we could fight back—in the manner of our patron Kali, the many-armed Hindu goddess of destruction, creation, and preservation.

Far too many women could use those extra arms. Every four minutes a man rapes a woman, author Kay Leigh Hagan recently reminded me in an interview. Hagan has researched the whole issue of violence against women in her book *Fugitive Information: Essays from a Feminist Hothead.* Every fifteen seconds a man beats a woman. Four out of five murdered women are killed by men— between a half and a third are married to their murderers, she said.

I confess I dream of owning a gun. I know this is not a politically correct fantasy. And yes, I know, I should sign up for a self-defense class. But in my fantasy I am so skilled with my little pearl-handled Beretta that I get the perpetrator—not the other way around.

Please don't cite all those statistics about how guns endanger the innocents more than the criminals. I know the numbers, and I am no fan of the National Rifle Association.

Instead, just take a moment to appreciate all the ways, big and small, women circumscribe their lives. I sympathize with those who live in high-crime neighborhoods. For women, our high-crime neighborhood is the world and, according to stats on domestic violence, our own homes.

I have become expert at eyeballing parking lots as I walk to my car, but one can see only so much. Evolution short-changed us again: We have no eyes in the backs of our heads.   ∎

1997

Saving Graces

My ears are red with fever. What started as a lump in my throat is now a bonfire in my lungs. I lie in bed and think about the vale of tears that is this world: hunger, disease, war. I call a friend and tell him, "It's useless, all useless."

He recommends a hot-water bottle. "So you feel like shit," he says. "Rent a horror movie and pop some popcorn."

As long as I'm miserable, I might as well enjoy it. Not one for horror films, I escape into a book about Aztec mythology. It tells about the deity Quetzalcoatl, who brought forth bones from the underworld that the goddess Cihuacoatl ground to a powder in a bowl. Other gods shed their blood in the bowl, and humans came into being.

I pick up a piece of paper and start jotting down words, forgetting about the fire inside, at least for now.

BRONCHITIS

Your voice, that red pickup truck
Loaded with opinions, weaves
On ice and flips into a ditch.
When you open your mouth
To say *help* you cough up
A feather from the plumed
Serpent, Quetzalcoatl.
The cops don't understand you.
The doctor says *breathe*
And you rattle and hiss.
Your grandmother warned

It could end this way:
Walking outside with
Damp hair, mal aire,
Bad air holding you
At gunpoint or worse.

Each inhale grinds
Your ribs to a powder.
You pray for nothing
Less than rebirth,
For health insurance,
As you tow the wreckage
Of your voice behind you
To the body shop
On Fourth Street.   ∎

2003

Birth Day

It's night, July 10, 1990—my thirtieth birthday. I'm inside a phone booth, hemmed in by Nevada desert, beneath a yellow moon. The man I married earlier today is with his brother in a barbeque joint from which I managed to escape with a lie, saying I had to call my mother. The number 0 on the telephone is an open mouth, shrieking a warning I can't make out. I'm shaking. A cold hand, or what feels like a cold hand, is pushing at my jaw, forcing me to look away from the phone.

Against my will I close my eyes and see the massive glass doors of the federal courtroom in Albuquerque, where I stood trial in 1988, accused of conspiracy against the United States, of smuggling Salvadoran refugees into the country as part of the Sanctuary Movement. I see myself on the witness stand speaking into a microphone—then I flash to the image of a machine gun in the hands of a soldier in El Salvador. Two years after my acquittal, I'm sure that I uttered something, I don't know what, that has led to the disappearance and death of someone in El Salvador.

I have not slept for three nights. Or has it been three weeks? I have tried and tried to look ahead to the rest of life, but how can I? I am among those damned for all time in a macabre dance of cause and effect. A butterfly flutters its wings and a tornado strikes, flattening a village. Two lovers couple and introduce AIDS to a continent. Sanctuary goes on trial in New Mexico, and a church worker in San Salvador has her name added to a government hit list.

And because I keep looking back, I am turning into a pillar of salt. My mind is exploding.

I reach for the phone, hit 0. Collect, I tell the operator. Norty, a doctor, a family friend, answers. "I don't know what's happening to me," I tell him. "I haven't slept for nights. . . . I'm afraid. The world seems to be going dark." My throat constricts. Now is the time to confess my crime, but I'm losing my nerve. I can't get the word "murderer" out of my mouth. *Sleep deprivation. Anxiety attacks. Depression.* I toss around clinical-sounding terms to cover up the blood on my hands and the chalk marks on the street outlining the body of the murdered Salvadoran church worker.

"Can you send me a few sleeping pills? A few nights of sleep and I'll be fine," I say.

Norty goes quiet. Then he begins a line of questioning I could never have anticipated. "Have you had any tendencies, as far as your moods go, towards highs and lows?" he asks. I pause. "Since I was a teenager," I say. "Maybe even earlier. But everyone has their ups and downs."

"Have these mood swings become more frequent or more pronounced?" he asks.

"If you put it that way . . . yes, I guess so. But right now I'm sure it's just the insomnia that's causing everything. Are you able to overnight a few pills to me?" I flash back again to the packed courtroom. The microphone. The machine gun. "You know how it is when you don't sleep."

But Norty won't bite. Instead, he drops a bomb: He thinks that I could be suffering from bipolar disorder, also known as manic-depression. He must have heard the desperate rasp in my voice, the death rattle. For a blessed moment I forget I'm on trial and remember previous waves of elation sweeping over me only to give way to sadness so black I could paint with it, my mind racing through the night with ideas for books to write, countries to visit, causes to embrace—only to detour down a dark alley of paranoia, dead-ending in paralysis.

Any sense of a center, or a stable identity, had long eluded me. Routines—the loom upon which one weaves a life—fell apart whenever I did.

But it had never occurred to me to blame an illness for chaos that was, in fact, payback from the universe. For all my outward successes, I had failed to cultivate equanimity. Other people seemed to pull it off, in varying degrees. They exercised, ate right, meditated, kept better schedules, chose more compatible partners, went into therapy, and above all, climbed into bed at the same time every night. They exercised willpower. They were better, stronger, more moral people. I moved among them with grace, a perfect fraud.

I do my best to say some of this to Norty, but my sentences snap in two, and I'm not sure I'm making sense. "I'm tired," I say. I see the figure of my husband in the distant barbeque joint beneath the noose of a moon. I have to admit to myself I've been exhausted. For years. Long before this terrible week of obsessively tending a corpse somewhere in El Salvador, which now my friend is suggesting might be a figment of my imagination.

Still there was more to my history, evidence of a different sort.

In July 1979, after my first year of college, I resumed my habits from adolescence of writing poetry or just sitting in silent meditation in my parents' backyard. For a month the world around me had appeared desolate, a wasteland abandoned by the heavens. But then one afternoon it began to shimmer. A gentle light encircled trees, plants, even stones. Time's rush collapsed into one present moment.

For over a month I saw this light emanating from people too. This was no heavenly event I experienced. The beauty I witnessed was in and of this earth. I imagined a day when this light would be visible to all. Who then could hate another person, or think of the earth as dead matter? We were born to live in wholeness. Catholicism echoed this intuition, this political vision, in a prayer: "As it was in the beginning, is now, and ever shall be, world without end."

I knew this experience was not unique to me; history is full of stories of sinners and saints alike who have achieved similar states with drugs, marathon running, monastic training, and the like. But that knowledge could not rob me of the utter wonder I beheld, and with it the growing conviction that a healed world was within our reach, if we could only remember what it looked like.

"Are you there?" Norty asks. I hesitate, taking a moment to honor that other birth day, even as I face the prospect that my brain's faulty wiring may have triggered my susceptibility to the light.

"Yes," I say.

Bipolar disorder. The words roll in my head like dice. What if this is my lucky day? What if I'm not a fraud, or a moral failure, but someone struggling with an illness? *The microphone? The machine gun?* What if I don't deserve the death sentence after all? Is it possible that in this glass confessional, I am being absolved?

"What should I do?" I ask. It's late; I've got to get back to the restaurant. "I'll fly you home," Norty says. He wants me to see a doctor of internal medicine, a man with a special interest in working with psychiatric patients. "I can last a few more days here," I tell him. I promise to set up an appointment right away. "Call collect at any hour if you need to talk," Norty says, "or if you change your mind about coming home."

That night I don't sleep but a few hours, yet my spirit rests. I can live with this suffering a few more days, because someone called it by its true name, called it out of the mists.

I look back at that night in Nevada and the years that led up to it; for all the horrors untreated manic-depression can visit upon a person, the story of my illness is in many ways unremarkable. I never jumped from a rooftop intending to fly, nor did I point the barrel of a gun at my tonsils. What I did do was point a pencil at a piece of paper.

In junior high I used to lie on the carpet or sit at the backyard picnic table and write about the day, or simply describe the wind and trees. In those days I was so shy I could hardly get a word out of my mouth. Yet words came forth from my hand, as if I were playing at a Ouija board that spelled out what I couldn't other-wise have known. During one of those sessions it came to me that I should write letters to myself. I would read these when sadness ("depression" was not so common a word back then) sucked the life out of me, leaving me unable at times to get out of bed. The letters contained to-do lists: Go visit a neighbor, cook a pot of soup, pray. I pleaded with myself to remember: "This is not your true self; this will pass." Above all, I ordered myself to write in my journal, a practice that would become second nature thanks to high school creative-writing classes.

Blank notebooks were a parallel universe I entered at will by lifting a pen. Merely entering the date and the year at the top of each page got my adrenaline up as over time my very body began to associate writing with surprises, with hope. Often, while listening to songs on the radio, I wrote out some of my favorite lyrics, forming lines and stanzas as I imagined the author had intended. The shapes of the words on the page were a pure pleasure to behold. I was especially taken by the work of Joni Mitchell. I had collected her albums. I studied her lyrics as they appeared on the inside of the cover. Each song was a world unto itself, complex and compelling. Using her melodies as a guide, I began to make up my own lyrics. I didn't think of this process as writing poetry until I began to write in stanzas without having to rely on another person's melodic structure. It was like removing training wheels from a bicycle and finding I could whiz forward all on my own.

My agonies, real or imagined, adolescent melancholia or blinding depression—all this raw feeling found expression, which is its own kind of resolution. Writing is no cure for mental illness, but keeping a journal was a way to step outside the violent whirlwind of my emotions so that I could watch. The observer in me—that is to say, my spirit—broke off from my manic-depressive mind, and it is to that observer that I owe my life.

Today, and quite likely for the rest of my life, I will swallow a handful of pills before bedtime. I'm lucky. The only side effect I've experienced is mental health. I have my ups and downs, but these tend to be of the garden variety, and are often related to dips in blood sugar, which I can control with a proper diet and exercise.

Meanwhile, knowledge of bipolar disorder grows exponentially, and the cool clinical ring of the label has removed some of the stigma of the disease, which afflicts an estimated 2.3 million American adults.

It has taken years to fine-tune my medications, an exhausting process. One's spirit must be alert at all times, watching the mind for signs of a coming storm. I've been known to appear at doctor's appointments with pages of notes; even mild mania or depression are states that for me can be impossible to recall once I've rejoined the living. Recording the experiences can be a great tool for tracking the frequency and intensity of episodes, as well as what triggered them.

With the fine-tuning of medications comes the challenge of learning to conduct one's life: cooking, sleeping, planning—all those life-giving routines that founder in times of chaos. Manic-depressives are used to weathering great crises of the spirit; it is another thing altogether to sit down, make a grocery list, and set a time to go to the store. I've often felt shame at having to undertake such baby steps at a late age, but I've found it's better to bless the shame than to fight it. Like any emotion, shame is a life form that, by definition, will fight to live; treating it like an enemy only energizes it. Acknowledge it with compassion, and it stops vying for attention. Such awareness teaches us finally to love ourselves, mental illness and all, a process that calls to mind Galway Kinnell's poem "St. Francis and the Sow," which speaks of the need to "reteach a thing its loveliness."

More than shame, grief was my companion in the wake of my diagnosis. This was good. I needed to grieve. Large portions of my life, it seemed, had disappeared. I wept for the aborted relationships and projects, for the deadness I often felt in the face of beauty. Too I grieved for the great stretches of my life that I could not recall, because I had been sleepwalking instead of truly living. I grieved that I had been unable to turn to my own family for help because I didn't know that what I was experiencing had a name.

During especially rough patches, I took consolation from the word "insane," because the word is ancient and richly evocative of so much of human suffering. "Insane" yokes me to the masses of those wounded to the core, and there is great consolation in knowing that I am not alone, that my plight is not unique. Our wounded world teems with people who have been disappeared: due to illness, abuse, war, poverty and the policies that perpetuate it, to tyranny of every sort. In the end, grieving freed me from remaining trapped in my personal story. I wiped my tears and looked around. I rejoined the human race.

It's a sunny afternoon in April 2004. Today there are only thirty-four people in front of me waiting to pick up their medicines at discount—not the more than sixty people waiting the Friday before the Martin Luther King holiday. We belong to a program, affiliated with a local hospital, that serves the indigent. A computer-generated voice says, "Now serving seven zero one at counter number four," then repeats the words in Spanish. We speak quietly in our pharmacy or not at all, fearful we'll miss hearing our number being called above the static cackle of a broken television set.

We are all colors, all ages, but in this modern-day breadline, we look alike. We are tired. Tired from working day shifts and graveyard shifts with no health insurance to show for it. Tired from looking for work, or working for nothing as we care for children and elderly parents. We're tired and dreading the day, once a year if not more often, when we have to gather pay stubs, utilities bills, proof of timely rental and house payments, costs of car insurance—adding and subtracting our existence to show that we haven't made a penny too much, thus disqualifying ourselves from this program. We're tired but grateful. At least we see doctors for a reasonable cost and can afford our meds. But fear lurks inside our gratitude that this safety net, like so many in the United States today, will shred beneath us, leaving us to drown.

I look around to see if I can spot one of my tribe. Manic-depressives: We are the ones whose spirits dribble out of us like blood; we're the artists of spirit retrieval. But one can sustain such heroics only so long. Without access to health care—a diagnosis and treatment—exhaustion will mete out its terrible sentence. Hence the disproportionate numbers of suicides among undiagnosed manic-depressives, or slow death by self-medication with alcohol and other drugs. As a self-employed writer, I can't afford the three-hundred-dollar-a-month cost of my meds, or visits to doctors to get refills. That's why I'm here. HMOs want nothing to do with me, a bipolar patient who despite her success with pills (no therapy, suicide attempts, hospital visits) is automatically classified as high risk, a threat to profits. I'm here because the few plans that would take me on cost so much that I'd have to cease making house payments, at which point I'd be sent away to enroll in the local health care for the homeless program.

Friends and family tell me that they will help me find a solution should I ever be bumped from the indigent program. But try telling that to the woman who still remembers the shrieking 0 of the phone in a booth in Nevada. Try telling that to the woman seated beside me, uninsurable because of lupus. I was saved by a collect call to a doctor friend, but salvation that is purely personal is a sham. The only solution to my problem is political: Health care, a basic human right, must be made available to all.

On a beautiful spring day in 2002, at a packed bookstore in Tucson, a man raises his hand and asks me, "Don't medications dull your creativity?" I'm taking questions after reading from a newly released book of poetry. Earlier in the week I had "come out" as a manic-depressive in an interview with a newspaper. I had decided it was time to roll away the stone of secrecy.

"Mental health does not dull creativity," I answer. "Mental illness does."

I try to explain. Severe depression chips away slowly, or bludgeons suddenly, one's desire to live and finally to write; to see this truth, one need only count the high rate of suicides among poets, or the abandoned manuscripts in the drawers of the quietly desperate. Kay Redfield Jamison powerfully documents this sad history in *Touched with Fire: Manic-Depressive Illness and the Artistic Temperament*.

Mania is no better. All too quickly the manic state—marked by insomnia, grandiose thoughts, and reckless behavior—turns to paranoia, irritability, self-loathing, panic, and mental gridlock. Sleep deprivation aggravates symptoms, threatening productivity, especially as one ages. Whatever elation one might have felt about commencing the great American novel morphs into its opposite, the "darkness visible" that William Styron writes so eloquently about in his book of that title.

The gentleman who asked the question is an artist. I hope he is not like so many, mostly male, artists I encounter who seem determined to go it alone—to quit their meds, romanticizing "madness" as a means to creativity.

We live in an insane and wounded world. We are sundered by borders of every sort. This is more than enough to inspire creative work. The resulting "psychic unease" that Gloria Anzaldúa describes in *Borderlands/La Frontera: The New Mestiza* can sharpen one's perceptions and one's pencil. In a similar vein, Alice Walker, in the title essay of *Anything We Love Can Be Saved,* writes that more and more people are struggling to "decolonize their spirits." All this is sacred work, political work, and the writer who takes it up will encounter no end of material for poetry, fiction, and nonfiction.

I've come to accept that I may never again see the light of the world as vividly as I did during the summer of 1979. The truth is, the brain is not wired to take in so much luminescence, much less a darkness that borders on the demonic. For a long time after those months, I felt abandoned by the gods, until I realized that my calling—the human calling—is to try to embody light in my life, most especially when I cannot see it. And to try to embody it in my writing as well.

You tell me there is a place
In the universe for those
Who wrestle with demons.
Tell me, what did the devil do

With my lost years?
Did he eat them?
Did he fall into a sound sleep
And so spare a single soul from pain?
I don't think so.
And why, all these years later,
Must I forgive him long enough
To touch with love
All that was lost,
Forgive myself
Long enough
To write these poems? ▪

2003–2004

Sign Language

Chalk it up to my bad habit of asking for signs. A friend called me on a recent Saturday afternoon. He'd been to a psychic who instructed him to tell me that I was cured. As we speculated on which of my maladies was no more, I heard what sounded like plaster falling from the ceiling. I got up from the living room rug, where I'd been basking in the sun like a cat. Phone in hand, I followed a mysterious trail of yellow goo to the dining room wall. Here I found an egg, shattered, its half shell stuck to the wall.

Where did the egg fall from? Heaven? I begged my friend to drive over and take a look. Objectivity was called for, and my brain is not wired to piece together evidence. I leap prematurely to myth and meaning, symbol and sign.

I thought of the use of eggs to bring about cures in Latino and Native American rituals. Elena Ávila, psychiatric nurse and curandera, often performs limpias, or spiritual cleansings, by sweeping an egg over a person's body. She sometimes cracks the egg in a bowl and, examining the configuration of its contents, "reads" a person's energy. All this is done with prayer, as she describes in her acclaimed book, *Woman Who Glows in the Dark: A Curandera Reveals Traditional Aztec Secrets of Physical and Spiritual Health.*

As a child, my sister would wrap refrigerated eggs in towels and put them in a kitchen drawer, sure that they would hatch. Her faith in miracles prefigured the birth of her own child after a long struggle with infertility. Her little girl's journey to this earth included a stay in a freezer during her time as an embryo and a flight (still frozen) to California, thanks to Airborne Express. It's not the nativity scene the pope has in mind. Now seven years old, Rachel will soon be preparing for First Holy Communion.

At last my friend arrived, walking in through the open screen door. I showed him the eggshell on the wall. I looked for the face of Jesus in the yellow drippings. No such luck. We studied the pattern of the goo on the floor. It seemed to point to the screen door, which I had left open all afternoon to bathe the house in the fresh autumn air.

Ah, so that was it! Some poor kid couldn't help himself. Some kid, with considerable eye-hand coordination, rolled that egg across my floor at lightning speed. I drew a deep breath then laughed as I pulled out the mop. Who was I to be angry? I had committed far worse sins in my youth because I couldn't help myself.

My miracle egg was not a miracle after all. Or was it? I am so used to reading about flying bullets and bombs that the egg renewed my faith in humankind. Somewhere some kid was chuckling on this glorious autumn day, telling his friends about the open door and a hole in one worthy of Tiger Woods. ▪

2003

Unsung Remedies

Too much daylight makes me frantic. Maybe this has to do with the years I lived beneath the merciless Tucson sun. Perhaps it has to do with being manic-depressive. Having suffered the extremes of dark and light, my kind often experience well-being in the shade: of a cottonwood tree or a trellis overgrown with morning glories; in a café but not by the window; in the kitchen where beans boil on the stove and blanket the windows in steam. We are drawn to Mexican lace, flowery sheers, bamboo, Venetian blinds, and Japanese screens: whatever materials allow us to play with light and thereby set our inner worlds aright.

Twilight is my favorite time of day. Here the gods themselves separate light from dark. Everything quiets down (or perhaps I do, and the outside world follows). It's a time of hushed, fresh beginnings. The day, with all its upsets, is over and done. I open my journal and take notes for a poem.

NIGHT OWL

Each evening you tear up
The suicide note, dry your
Eyes, write a five-year
Plan for your life, do
Your nails, then clean
And soak the beans.
To passersby your house
Looks like a luminaria, lit
From within by candles,
And the slow burn of lamps,

A TV, and the blue
Flame of the gas stove.

You're in your element.
The happiest day of the year
Is when you turn back
The clock and dip the day
In darkness like a strawberry.

The light of day is ruthless.
The sun a bloody sore.
Each ring of the phone
Is a grenade going off.
The curtains hang useless
As old bandages.
You close your eyes
But your brain's grid
Grinds on, powered
By a star. ▪

2003–2004

Columnas Culturas

Confessions of a Berlitz-Tape
Chicana

Confessions of a Berlitz-Tape Chicana

We're everywhere, and it's time to come out of the closet: I speak of the tongue-tied generation, buyers of books with titles like *Master Spanish in Ten Minutes a Day while You Nap.* We're the Chicanas with cassettes in our glove compartments; commuting to work, we lip phrases for directing an Argentine cabbie to a hotel or ordering tapas at a bar in Spain.

At home we flip through catalogs of classes offered abroad. We imagine acquiring the language the way we might a wardrobe. But it costs: tuition for language school, tickets to Guatemala, and a pair of Birkenstocks. It costs to be among the linguistic tourists my dad calls "Sandalistas."

Yet how seductive. Total immersion! In a foreign country! So go the testimonies of our friends, long after they've forgotten most of what they learned.

But we know better. We live, after all, in occupied Mexico—and beyond, in every U.S. barrio and 'burb where Latinos reside. We show up with potato salad and tamales at raucous family affairs that make even funerals worth the tears. Here we encounter aunts with names like Consuelo, Elvira, and Maudi, and uncles Bamba, Elfigo, and Juan. After lunch they sink into couches and eat cake off paper plates. They speak a thick and sweet Spanish, marbled with English. Total immersion? No place like home.

Meanwhile, cousins cluster together and renew our vows to work at our Spanish. We grew up listening to the language—usually in the kitchens of extended family—but we answered mostly in English. We refer to our "broken" Spanish as if it were a broken bone and speak of how, when we least expect it, the language "comes back" as if it were a preexisting condition.

We are ashamed, for something precious shattered under our watch. And we are determined. We want our children to achieve a fluency we still struggle for. After my niece Rachel was born, I repeatedly recited the Our Father to her. Danos hoy el pan de cada día; give us this day our daily bread. I wanted to begin, day one, to open her neuropathways not merely to God, but to the Spanish language.

My own education in Spanish began the first year of my life, when my father was stationed in Okinawa. My mother and I lived with her parents, who daily crisscrossed the border between Spanish and English as they talked politics and poker. Later on, my father's parents took me to the church of the First Spanish Assemblies of God. Here, God made his glory known, not only in tongues but also in Spanish, through the voice of a preacher who pointed at the Bible, thundered, and wept. My ears were opened: At dinners afterward, I huddled with my cousin at the edge of adult conversation. We knew what the grown-ups were saying when they switched to Spanish to talk about grown-up things.

At home, on the telephone, Dad breezed in and out of Spanish, his inflections bending this way or that depending on whether he was talking to an elder from northern New Mexico or an old buddy from the barrio. I don't remember my mom speaking much Spanish; an introvert, overwhelmed perhaps by my father's abilities, Spanish resided in her ear and not so much on her tongue.

The children in the neighborhood and in elementary school spoke English, with few exceptions. So did the children on television: the *Brady Bunch,* the *Partridge Family.* Fifth grade, however, brought a surprise: A girl from Puerto Rico joined the class. We became friends. I flexed my Spanish, she her English; we firmed up our linguistic muscles until, one day, she moved away.

That same year I wrote a paper and used a word my teacher said didn't exist. I'd always earned high marks for writing. Teachers said my comprehension of the English language was advanced for my age—in no small part, I believe, because my mother took me to the local library more often than to church.

I pointed to the word in the dictionary; the teacher concurred. This incident seems important—it is still so vivid. That obscure English word, so obscure I can't recall it, was not only a word, it was a way: command of the English language and its shadow side—command over others. At the time all I knew was the thrill of having "discovered" a word. It would be years before I would grasp the politics of the tongues in which we speak and witness the privilege heaped upon those who can wield English like a sword.

On weekends I spent the night with my maternal grandmother. She used to draw herself up to her full height and order, not ask, my father, "Déjala, déjala," she'd say, let her—referring to me—let her eat that candy, stay over another night, jump on the bed. Dad shrank in silence. Grandma cast her spell with a Spanish word that signified unconditional love.

My father was elected to the Albuquerque school board in 1969, the first Chicano to hold this position; this in the wake of the passage of a landmark piece of legislation, the Bilingual Act of 1967. My father would enter the great debates of the day, debates that have never ceased. One camp saw the use of Spanish as a mere stepping stone to mastering English. The camp to which my father belonged envisioned the classroom as a place where a child would achieve fluency in two languages.

Dad insisted I take Spanish when junior high and high school rolled around. I aced my classes. "Your accent is perfect," my teachers purred. In college I studied more, having tested into an advanced class.

After graduating, I went on to read the great Spanish-language poets, from Gabriela Mistral to César Vallejo, in long ecstatic stretches every morning on the plaza of Old Town, Albuquerque. I listened to the gossip of the viejitas as they emerged from morning mass at San Felipe Church. I yearned to ask them how long they'd lived on this eighteenth-century plaza, how life had changed. But the tide of spoken English was too strong. By the time I translated what I wanted to say in my head, they'd moved on.

Yet with time, that yearning has gotten the better of me. I go longer and longer periods now conversing in Spanish, forgetting I'm "not fluent"—which may be one definition of fluency.

One afternoon, I found myself in the orange groves outside Phoenix; here Guatemalan refugees lived under the trees until they could get a ride with a coyote to Florida. Churches brought meals. A mobile medical clinic rolled in. Exhausted women lined up. A nurse handed me a clipboard. We're short, she said, can you do intake? My lungs filled like sails. I asked the women when they had their last period. I asked them about their journey. My tongue was untied.

Another scene comes to mind: I am walking through Harvard Yard with a poet from Vietnam. "Beautiful night" is about all we say to one another before we fall silent. Then he turns to me and asks, in Spanish, "Do you speak Spanish?" "Yes," I answer, "where did you learn yours?" "In Cuba," he says. We talk on. Our words are like pieces of a child's puzzle that we put together to make a picture of our lives.

In 2001 the Salvadoran novelist Manlio Argueta invited me to his country for a conference on testimonial literature after the Salvadoran civil war. He asked me to talk about my novel, *Mother Tongue,* which tells the story of a Salvadoran refugee and his Chicana lover. The book is set during the Sanctuary Movement of the 1980s, when U.S. citizens defied immigration law by opening their homes to Guatemalan and Salvadoran refugees.

I wrote out my presentation in Spanish, no problem. The legacy of the tongue-tied is that the unsaid often rushes, with a weird ease, to our hands and then to the page. Those years of in-class writing assignments surely helped. Yet as in the orange groves outside Phoenix and in Harvard Yard, a yearning to connect had me fumbling, joyously, for the right word, or even the next best word. Yearning cuts through fear of the next best word, of imperfection. And it cuts through guilt and shame.

Guilt crops up when we tell ourselves: I'm Latina, I should be fluent. Shame follows when we're around the fluent and afraid to speak up. So powerful are these emotions that it does no good to know that much in our history has conspired against fluency, English Only movements being but one especially virulent manifestation. Who hasn't heard a story, recalled by elders or even contemporaries, of punishments meted out for speaking Spanish in school, from mouths washed out with soap to placement of Spanish speakers in classes for the mentally handicapped?

And some of our own are our worst enemies: the more-Chicano-than-thou and more-Mejicana-than-thou intellectuals and activists who look down on the rest of us—perhaps because we reflect so explicitly their own struggle to find their voices.

Once I participated in a panel at the Smithsonian with Puerto Rican poet Martín Espada and Claribel Alegría of El Salvador. A woman in the audience stood up and accused: How dare we speak as Latinos about Latino literature—in English?

I have long maintained that Spanish is a father tongue, that of the conquerors. Our true mother tongues are indigenous languages, many wiped out in the genocide. I dream of a day when we Latinos are trilingual, or at least studying a third tongue. Quechua, Tewa, Yoheme, Diné, Nahuatl—the roads to recovery are legion. I managed to convey something like this, even as I felt a sword had been aimed at my throat.

One of the protagonists of *Mother Tongue* is Soledad, godmother to María, who is the lover of José Luis of El Salvador. Soledad smuggles Central American refugees into the United States and dispenses advice to María about everything from life outside the law to home remedies. When she gets wind of María and José Luis's love affair, she counsels, in a letter to her goddaughter: "Mijita, if you must lose your head over that boy, at least apply yourself and use the experience to shore up your Spanish. How do you think I learned English? Remember that good-for-nothing first husband I once told you about? Well, we were young and in love and what he said when we were together needed no translation. Falling in love with a man who speaks another language, you develop a third ear. First, you struggle to understand what he says. Then you begin to hear what he means. Then the relationship falls apart. But you're the better for it." She ends the letter, "Write soon—in Spanish. If you don't know a word, make it up."

Awash in the music of Spanish, my generation grew a third ear. We fell in love with what we heard. That love drives us out of our solitude. "I want to rediscover the secret of great speech and of great burning," writes Aimé Césaire in *Notebook of a Return to the Native Land.* "I want to say storm. I want to say river." We tongue-tied possess the secret of great speech and burning. Tempestad, río. Word by word, we're making our way back home. ▪

2003

By Any Other Name

Latina? Chicana? Mejicana? Mexican American? Nuevo Mejicana? The name of choice among many progressive intellectuals is "Latina/o"—a rejection of "Hispanic," a word that Europeanizes us, an appendage of the days when we meekly answered "Spanish" when our elementary school teacher inquired about our ethnic identity.

"Latina" did not at first suggest for me a linkage to our indigenous and African roots. The word takes us back to Rome and the languages that developed from Latin, such as Italian, French, and Portuguese as well as Spanish. However, "Latina" has come to mean so much more as growing numbers claim the word with pride. We can't be pushed to the back of the bus because we fill too much of it. Over the code-switching radio DJ, we speak English with Salvadoran, Nuyorican, Cuban and other accents. Whatever our ethnic differences, we are family!

Lately, when asked, I have tended to say that I'm Mexican. I like the word because it still makes so many people flinch. "Mexican" was, and still is, a dirty word in the racist lexicon. Even some of our own people, who identify as Hispanic, speak disparagingly of "Mexicans"—newcomers to this side of the border. Historical memory, so precious, pales when people start scaling the social ladder.

Nothing is fixed. In the name game, improvisation is the magic word. I'm a Latina to promote pan-American unity. A Nuevo Mejicana to specify place and ancient ties to the land. I'm a Chicana as a result of the great "naming ceremony" of which Rudolfo Anaya writes—the adoption of the name by Chicano movement activists who were determined to honor their long-reviled indigenous roots. And I'm Mexican American, a handy way to refer to the largest Latino subgroup in the United States.

Finally, I'm Hispanic among those who couldn't care less about the debate over naming but who know they'd better get out and vote because right now they are screwed: low wages, substandard education, no health insurance, over-represented in prisons and in military uniforms. They know the rich and powerful will skewer the poor, by whatever name. ∎

2003

Trickle Up

Every Latino poet I know struggles with the question of how best to take the fruits of our solitude into the public square. That we must work out our individual destinies in relationship to our communities, as activists and artists, is a given. Whether reading from our works or speaking out on an issue, we try to voice our concerns from the heart, sharing our passion with others, abandoning the jargon we may have mastered in academia, in order to be heard by as many as possible.

We are among the privileged. We are literate in a world where the vast majority of people are condemned to illiteracy, the poor of whom Eduardo Galeano writes in his essay "In Defense of the Word." To speak of this unspeakable situation—to bear witness, to propose alternatives—demands that we spend our lives listening, really listening, to those who suffer because of inhuman policies perpetrated by governments and corporations alike. Latin America's liberation theology insists upon the centrality of story, of the need for poor people to tell of their plight in their own words. Having told their own stories, they can then go on to interpret their reality, and develop plans of action, in light of the biblical vision of justice on earth. Only by learning to be present, to really listen to the stories and analyses of the poor, do we earn the right to lift up their concerns from our places of privilege.

I've become wary of North American distortions of liberation theology. I hear many well-meaning religious progressives talk of speaking out "on behalf of the poor" or for those "who have no voice." I find this highly problematic. Whatever speaking out we do must be *with* the poor. No one lacks a voice. Not even the dead. But many lack ears, the ability to hear those stories out of which the most destitute of people are forging their destinies, breathing life into bleached bones. ∎

2004

Spirit Matters

Writers are contemplatives. Daily we give ourselves over to silence, only to find the world at its worst marching across the snowy horizon of the page. The characters one had such hope for turn out to be, well, human. They hate, manipulate, seduce other people's spouses. They love money, worry about their looks, and fume about the state of the nation while making no effort to change things.

This is not to say that grace does not happen in their lives, instances of beauty and truth, wee epiphanies that unleash desire to live for . . . something more, something the world's religions have named variously as compassion, agape, wakefulness, tikkun, the call to repair the earth. But all it takes is a traffic jam, a bad hair day, and my characters—those mirrors of my own heart—forget, entering once again into what Buddhism calls maya, illusion, or what Christians call sin.

Still, the novelist hopes. We watch our characters without judgment, embracing equally what is lovely and what is sinister. We hope that in the end they will learn something about life and love—that is, if the darkness they court does not swallow them up first.

At times we try to push our creations toward safety and right action. But souls, even fictional ones, are not so easily manipulated. Like a parent, the novelist must eventually get out of the way so that characters can become their own persons, enter into their own pacts with God and the devil. Chapter by chapter, our characters teach us that few people are wholly good or wholly evil. The writer who cannot love the color gray, who cannot embrace a world that is anything but black and white, will not last long. Our creations will die for lack of compassion if we replace truth telling with moralizing.

I'm not sure what any of this has to do with God or spirituality. Those words, bandied about so readily, frighten me even as they draw me like a moth to fire. I'm always amazed by the number of artists I know who once dreamed of becoming priests or nuns, myself included. It seems, however, that in reaching for heaven, we fell all the harder back to earth.

The novelist is condemned to earth. We are called to be faithful not to abstract doctrine, so vaunted by organized religion, but to what our five senses tell us about the world around us. We may be affiliated with religions that preach a loving, all-powerful, and just God, but we are not God's public relations flacks. In our writing we must be willing to indict God, to tell the other side of the story. We tell stories as we find them—of the war veteran, the refugee, the diseased, the lonely, the insane. The novelist begs for an answer to the question, "Where were you, O God?" We leave it to theologians to formulate answers. Our work is to stand in solidarity with those who have no answers.

When our characters experience what seems to be the presence of the sacred in a moment of healing, heroism, cleansing anger, or bliss, we tell that story, too. For who is not to say that the world as a whole is not struggling to realize a greater experience of the sacred? The writer's imagination must be roomy and supple enough for hope and joy as well as gloom and doom.

Our imaginations must be on call at all times, open to any possibility. So we fight sloth and fear and struggle to show up each day before the blank page. If a writer can be said to have a spiritual practice, this is it: to stay awake until the imagination stirs and music comes out of our hands. My hope is that by writing well, I will help keep you, the reader, awake—and in love with the human project despite the tumultuous times in which we live. ■

1996

Pointers

Many people, particularly poets, have asked me for tips on how to write a novel. I wrote my novel, *Mother Tongue,* in a nine-month trance while working at a full-time job. I had never taken a fiction workshop. Had I known what I was doing, I might never have done it. I pressed on only because of an abiding faith that the story was already finished, afloat in the universe—all that the universe was asking of me was to take the story down.

Far from home, in Kansas City, Missouri, I nourished myself on memories of New Mexico and recreated them in the book. (Some days I even put a green chile in the toaster oven so that the scent could transport me back.) I never tried to approach the book as a novelist, which I don't think I am, but as a poet. Following are a few pointers, based upon one poet's experience, that I hope will demystify the process:

1. Write one paragraph, long or short, each day on one sheet of paper. Write it with the care and precision with which you would write a stanza of a poem. The only difference is that you're not doing line breaks. When in doubt, describe an object, place, or person. Make it shine. Make it new. Fidelity to the simple act of description opens the way for insight, meaning, connections that should surprise you, the author, and, ultimately, the reader.

2. Save up these sheets of paragraphs. Depending on whether you write every day or not, you could have over three hundred in a year. Unless you feel so moved, don't number them. You'll know when the time is right to toss the pages in the air and see where they land. To discover what order they want to be in, as demanded

by the story itself. Each precious sheet of paper is a block for a quilt that you must trust will reveal its ultimate pattern.

3. When in doubt, go to a store with a fine collection of fiction and browse for hours. Find the slenderest volumes and rest assured: Telling the truth does not always require many words. Juan Rulfo's *Pedro Páramo*. *The Lover* by Marguerite Duras. Anything by Michael Ondaatje. *The Mixquiahuala Letters*, by Ana Castillo. The list is long, and I promise you, if you're receptive, the book you need to catapult you past your fears will all but fall off the shelf and into your hands.

4. Show up every day (or every other day, even though you risk losing momentum) at the page or screen for a minimum of fifty minutes. Set the oven timer. Think, women, of all meals you have cooked for others in that oven. What is fifty minutes? (I wrote *Mother Tongue* in daily fifty-minute segments, took Saturday off, and then resumed, for several hours, on Sundays.) Show up at the time you have scheduled. If you don't keep your date with the muse, she'll give up on you. You'll have to court her all over again, which takes time and energy.

5. Jump-start the senses when you prepare to sit down and write: candles, tea, incense, music, bowing to your computer—whatever turns you on. Rituals signal to the body that it's time to write. They cut way down on the amount of time we spend sitting, horrified, in front of the blank page. Figure out what practices work for you and before long, you will find you take to the page or the keyboard on cue, like an Olympic swimmer to water at the start of a race.

6. Read and write poetry. I could have accomplished none of the above if I had not worked on my poetry every day for years, and through many dry spells. We must be hunters and gatherers of words and images, so that when inspiration strikes, we have the raw materials needed to build the larger story that has presented itself to our imaginations.

7. Eat well and get sufficient sleep. Avoid alcohol and too much caffeine. We are physical beings, our imperfect bodies a miracle of circuitry for transforming impressions into words. To

create is to play with fire, to stand in a lightning field. Well-being and centeredness can keep us from burning up and burning out.

Above all, we must heed the advice author Grace Paley gave last summer at the William Joiner Center for the Study of War and Social Consequences. She told participants at the annual writing conference: "You can't always count on knowing what you're doing."

She spoke of searching through some old notes that she had once thought were worth nothing. She went on to make stories out of them. "I didn't know I had a vein of gold," she said of the notes. "I didn't even know I was in a mine." ∎

2003

Tortillas to You, Too

Two white male reviewers said that Latino identity appeared to be of little or no concern in my book *The Devil's Workshop*. I suspect this is because I did not write a poem about Jesus appearing on a tortilla. In fact, Chicana identity is everywhere in these poems, as necessary to their life as oxygen, even if invisible to some eyes. My obsessions with our medicinal traditions, our linguistic inheritance, and the U.S.–Mexico border are evident throughout the book. Other poems reflect upon the effects of war (Kosovo and Vietnam). Still others celebrate the births of my nephews, inspired by the Aztec tradition of prayer poems recited upon the birth of a child. As Chicana and Chicano writers, our only obligation is to tell our truths as beautifully as we can and in so doing join the global chorus of voices writing out of their histories and their hopes.

Still, I am waiting for Jesus, for anyone, to appear on my tortilla. Who, after all, can't use a sign?

HOUSEWARMING

You burn a corn tortilla
On the new gas stove.
You look for the face
Of Jesus but you've skipped
Mass too many times,
Dabbled in Eastern thought.
Instead you get a mandala:
Gold spokes shoot out
From a charred hub
Into eternity.

At the very least Mary
Should have appeared.
You want the real thing.
Guadalupe refrigerator
Magnets aren't good enough.
But you, my friend, are
The real thing:
Buddhalupe,
JesusKrishna.
The inquisitors
Flee when you
Finger the flame
And do not burn. ▪

2004

Sweet Revenge

"The best revenge is a book of poems," I tell high school girls who ask for advice on how they, too, can become writers. "Hold off on relationships. Concentrate on your studies. Write in your journal every day. Carry poetry in your knapsack, not beauty magazines." A serial marrier, I tell them, "Do as I say, not as I did."

We see it everywhere: Women's identities "disappeared" when they fall in love, even if a man doesn't want this kind of false sacrifice. Or women abandoning their own artistic pursuits to play muse to male artists, their lives frozen in the gaze of a painter, unable to reach for her star.

THE MUSE

It's the Catholic
Aztec in you:
This faith
In sacrifice,
This cutting
Open of what
Is ripe, bearing
All for the sake
Of the Sun.

He dips his pen
In your heart
And writes on.

To every woman I say, become your own muse. Write on: against the fear of being alone, against accusations of selfishness.

Write your way free of anyone else's expectations and into your own truth. Cultivate your talents. The truth is, you have no contract with men, but you have one with God. ∎

2003–2004

Bless You, Ultima

I was twelve years old when my father announced that to truly grasp New Mexico, I must read two books: *The Milagro Beanfield War,* by John Nichols, and *Bless Me, Ultima,* by Rudy Anaya.

With great pride Dad produced from his shelves a black book with an arresting image of a face: half woman, half owl. It was 1972, one year after Quinto Sol Publications in Berkeley had released *Ultima,* and Dad had read his personally autographed copy in record time. He emerged from the whirlwind with a message for me: Someone just like us, a Chicano, a New Mexican, had written and published a book, a book that told the truth about the place we inhabit, and how the spirit of this place inhabits us.

Thus began my introduction to Chicano literature, interrupted by four years at college and resumed upon my return home, where I forgot everything I ever learned about political economy and took up the craft of writing.

By then, Rudy Anaya had penned still more books. To say he was a role model for those of us Chicanos and Chicanas yearning to write would be an unforgivable understatement. He was more than that. He, like Ultima, had become an archetype. His mere presence among us emboldened us to reimagine New Mexico to our heart's delight, to find the words to give shape to our visions.

I don't use the word "presence" lightly. Rudy has personally mentored countless emerging writers. He has honored us by showing up at readings and political events. I remember so well the day of my arraignment in December 1987. That day court officers fingerprinted me, put me in a cell, lost me, found me, then released me to a packed courtroom. The first person I laid eyes on as I walked out was Rudy. I knew then and there that Nuevo Mejico stood behind my codefendant and me. I knew our community would keep us strong enough to see us through to victory.

Years later I had published my first collection of poetry and a novel, and a new collection was under way. Famous for their generosity to writers, Pat and Rudy had offered use of a casita they owned at the time in Jemez Springs. I'd signed up for a week, and aside from chasing off neighbors' goats that ate through one of Pat and Rudy's apple trees, my time was my own. Surrounded by red bluffs and hot springs, I finished my book.

I know I speak for a generation of writers when I say to Rudy, thank you. You listened when the call came for someone—someone just like us, as Dad said thirty years ago—to dream a New Mexico we could recognize as our own. We owe you a debt we can never pay back, except, God willing, with the words we write for the living and those yet to come. May you and Pat continue to bless us many long years with your words and your presence. ▪

Presented at the University of New Mexico in honor of Rudolfo Anaya, recipient of a 2001 White House Medal of Arts.

La Música

My muse is not Greek. She is not one of the nine daughters of Mnemosyne and Zeus, each of whom presided over a different art and science. The spirit that guides me is La Llorona, the Weeping Woman.

Her legend has been passed down in the Americas for hundreds of years, always shifting shapes, but it usually boils down to the tale of a woman haunting a river, crying out for her dead children.

Some, reading Spanish interpretations of pre-Columbian myths about a weeping woman, have suggested that the tale foreshadows the slaughter of the Aztecs by the conquistadores. Others say the story is about a woman who murdered her infant children after a lover abandoned her. Prophet of the conquest or mad woman driven to kill, Chicanos everywhere have feared and revered her. They've written scholarly papers about her and even warned their children to behave lest La Llorona appear at the window.

"Ay, mis hijos," my children, she wails down the corridor of the centuries. La Llorona is the Chicana poet's muse: She is a woman who will not be silenced. Her grief is as cosmic as her fury, regret, apocalyptic vision, and above all her yearning to tell her side of the story. She is every woman, dead and alive, hell-bent on testifying, from the murdered maquiladora workers of Juárez to the poet fidgeting with a pencil in a café, staring at a photograph of a Sudanese refugee.

Abandoned by a lover? Call La Llorona and she will take you walking along the Rio Grande after dark, her arm around your waist. I know. She's come calling for me whenever love has died in my hands like a sparrow and I've run out of friends to repeat the story to. We go out under the cottonwoods, remove our shoes, and step into the water. The tears of all humanity swirl around our ankles. We dip our hands in and taste the blood and salt of sorrow.

One night I tried to talk, to tell her about my failed love. I didn't want a ceremony. I wanted a tranquilizer: explanations with which I could cast blame upon the one who had left me. But La Llorona shushed me. "It's too early to trust words," she said. "Your work is to feel—and not only your own pain but that of others." We walked on. She cradled in her arms, in a black rebozo, all that I was not ready to say. She held me up as I cried out for my dead children, my dreams and delusions of love. I feared I was going mad—loca—a condition I knew too well in its chemical incarnation, but she was not moved. "So go mad," she said. "Haven't we all? I will be here to bring you back from the brink."

One night I waited for her as usual on my front porch, but she did not show up. I knew this could only mean one thing. I went back inside. On my desk I found, wrapped in a black rebozo, some paper, the kind the Aztecs made out of wild fig trees and the bark of mulberry. Amatl, it is called. "Llorona, Llorona," I whispered. What did she want me to write? How would I give form to our nights of ghostly wailing? Would I, as in the past, write an angry breakup poem—another x-ray of the heart where the most damage is done? Or could I write out of a spirit of reconciliation? What if this ending marked not disaster but transition and even healing?

What had gone unsaid for months began to spill onto the page. When the poems were done, I read them out loud on my front porch at midnight, facing the river. La Llorona's dead child, this one, was coming back to life.

CHANGES

I divide like a cell.
There goes my other half.
I don't go chasing.
I pour some tea
And entertain

A thought.
What if this is the way?
We fatten on love,
Find the wet pearl,
The wise word,
Then split off.
Cry as we might,
We are new.
I am done with
The myth of the
Broken heart.
A different story
Is taking root
For which I don't
Yet have the words.

WEDDED

The wall that separates us
Is the wall that weds us.

Straw bale, plaster, wire.
You can keep me out
But not the memory of sandhill cranes
That landed on diamond waters
At Bosque del Apache,
The sun bleeding into night.

For the fun of it I fold my heart
Like a paper airplane and send it
Whizzing over the wall.
Pick it up. Look at it.
Or you'll end up reading it in a book.

I've always said a poem is the best revenge.
But it's not revenge I desire.
Only that the wall come down,

And we replant the cottonwood
That was there before the bulldozer,
There even before love's enchantments.

Love? It's justice we must seek,
The act, whatever it is, that might make us whole.

THE BONESETTER

Do my tears frighten you?
Taste them. They have turned into wine.
Do I talk in my sleep?
Now yours is the name that I call out.

When you walked out, did you close the door gently?
No, but no matter. My house is not made of cards.
It stands, beautiful as a ruin, overlooking the city.

You call me up but I'm not home.
I'm back to my rounds, with bandages and muds,
In forgotten villages of northern New Mexico.

I am the huesera, the bonesetter.
I know the puzzle of the bones,
The song of the marrow.
I give up on no one, not even you.

I have spent my life holding what is broken,
Calling spirits back into bodies.

Does my strength scare you?
Come close. That's no storm you hear, just a breeze,
And the chimes the sound of your own voice. ∎

2003–2004

Bendita Soy Yo

Every night now I fall asleep reading Spanish: *Vivir Para Contarla,* Gabriel García Márquez's memoir; the fifty-cent *Hispano Times* out of Amarillo; the Nuevo Testamento, you name it. I rarely have bad dreams when I do this, perhaps because reading in another language is a sort of meditation: One slows down, thinking takes on the quiet patter of a gentle rain. I'm not sure why I continue to refer to Spanish as "another" language. With each new experience of it, Spanish becomes more and more my own, mi tierra. I can dispense of my passport and roam freely.

SONG

Bendito, bendito, bendito sea Dios
Los angeles cantan y alaban a Dios
Los angeles cantan y alaban a Dios
—ancient hymn of praise

Hold fast to the reins of Cervantes
When death closes in.
Spanish? That's an Arabian
Horse you're riding!
You say, Dios mío: my God,
Ojalá: I hope. But listen,
It's Allah you're hoping in,
Your horse resting in
The shadow of a tiled arch
A prayer away from the mosque.
My language is so close

To God it doesn't matter
If you believe or not.
For now death has given
Up on you. These words
Never will.   ▪

2004

The Passion

A few years back, during Lent, I had a dream. When I woke up, I recorded it exactly as I remembered it, with no embellishments, in the form of a poem.

UPON WAKING, A LENTEN DREAM

I walk to the front of a synagogue, take a seat.
(You cross your arms, stay standing in back.)
The congregants line up, come forward.
A rabbi smudges a circle of ash on each forehead.
I am thinking: I already received ashes on Wednesday.
I am thinking: I didn't know the Jews had such a
    ceremony.
I am thinking: Why am I surprised? So much of what we
    imagine
We invented was in fact inherited from the Jews.
Then a cantor, a woman, approaches me.
She opens a tin of honey, holds out the lid.
Taste, she says, and I touch the gold liquid, touch my
    tongue.
Before she moves on, she says, "You must learn
To accept sweetness as you have accepted ashes."
(And you? As always you stand detached.
Evading. Avoiding. The honey. The ash.)

So, it's not enough: to receive the ashes, to ponder our own inevitable deaths, to remember those who died at the hands of death squads or SS guards or those incinerated by bombs in

Hiroshima and Nagasaki. We ponder, remember, and repent, but we don't stop there. We taste the honey, celebrating the sweetness of life witnessed in a kind act, a work of art, the sky on a beautiful day, an unexpected victory in the struggle for justice. We honor the dead by celebrating life, loving it so deeply that we find it within ourselves to create a world without holocausts. Sin? We sin when we "stand detached," imagining we are above needing others. Only in community do we have the fortitude to partake of both ash and honey, and to cultivate the imagination we need to transform this earth.   ∎

2004

The Divine Mother

God or Goddess? I have long been uneasy with either name for the Divine. It's my own prejudice, of course, but God and Goddess sound too much like king and queen, figureheads whose faces are obscured by the height of their thrones and glare of their crowns.

But now, having journeyed back to New Mexico—for reasons I wouldn't have connected with religion—I have embraced a name for the sacred that I can live with: the Divine Mother.

One beautiful September night I found myself placing before a painting of the Virgin of Guadalupe a corsage I had sported earlier in the evening. I stepped back and gazed at her Buddha-like smile, her brown hands pressed together in prayer, her Aztec belt indicating pregnancy, and the gold aura enveloping her body. It was as if I had never seen her before, even though she appears everywhere—tattooed on the arms of prisoners, carved out of cottonwood, painted on the walls of restaurants; given a blank surface, her devotees will find a way to enshrine her.

I glanced again at the corsage. Stories locked in the periphery of my consciousness came forth: my mother, on the occasion of her high school graduation and later, her wedding, taking flowers to the statue of Mary at St. Vincent Academy in Albuquerque. And my grandmother with her parents, participating in pageants, in villages south of Albuquerque, in which Mary played the starring role.

On the feast day of St. Anthony, patron of Los Lentes village, a statue of Mary was carried in procession from house to house, my grandmother said. Mary was "visiting the community." The people recited rosaries and sung ancient songs of praise, or alabados. The owners of each house burned special incense on charcoals, adding rosebuds and sugar to the flame. Everybody feasted and drank pure cold water ladled out of a bucket drawn from the well.

Neither God nor Goddess, but something else: a Divine Mother brought down to earth by the devotion of the community; not devotion in the abstract, but a rich expression engaging all the senses, an opening of doors, a bienvenida and mi casa es tu casa.

Amazing what happens when you keep the door unlocked and the incense burning.

Just the other day the Divine Mother appeared in the person of a friend struggling to raise her children while holding down a low-paying job. We railed against deadbeat dads, evil landlords, and tax cuts for the rich. We conspired to seek out a lawyer who would take on a case against the father, pro bono. We conjured up a way for her to avoid a late fee on her rent. We imagined a day when things would be vastly different.

The spirit of the Magnificat filled the room. "The Almighty has done great things for me. . . . He has cast down the mighty from their thrones and has lifted up the lowly. He has filled the hungry with good things, and the rich He has sent away empty."

Surely Christianity's greatest mandate is that we must see Christ in all people. But sometimes Mary emerges as the more visible in the face of a woman. That is her great gift to a world that has rendered too many women faceless, voiceless, and powerless.

It might seem odd to some, this devotion to the Divine Mother on the part of a forty-three-year old woman—childless by choice.

Since I was a child myself, I'd known I did not want children of my own. In my teens, I sensed motherhood was not my calling. In my twenties, I made the decision to give birth in other ways: to books and to a life of activism.

In my early thirties, I learned that an anticonvulsant medication I take for bipolar disorder can cause a birth defect in which a child is born without a brain. Today I hear of friends' struggles as they make last-ditch efforts to conceive. Yet I never felt I was missing out on something. It was as if the Creator forgot to set the alarm on my biological clock.

The men who run the church would have me feel like the odd woman out. They offer no blessings to the millions who have discerned that motherhood is not our calling. Instead, they issue dire warnings against birth control. Catholics quietly "break the rules" or dribble out of the church rather than have their intelligence—indeed, their God—insulted.

Against this backdrop I have watched Latina friends, left and right, abandon Catholicism for Buddhism, where many have found a true home. I might have followed them but for the miraculous appearance of the Divine Mother in the mirror. I see myself in her light, loved. She affirms that all women (and men) who hew to the path of truth are giving birth. We are worthy of the Aztec belt and can proclaim, "From this day all generations will call me blessed."

I, too, am part of the Holy Family, la familia sagrada, in a way I always wanted to be: the crazy "spinster" aunt (to a niece and two nephews) whose bed is piled high with books, a sanctuary for any child who needs to be read to. ■

2003

Hola, Mary

I had no idea what I was doing—and had no business doing it.

Late one night I set out in search of a radio station over the Internet.

I had in mind some obscure broadcast emanating from the foggy highlands of Peru or the smoggy depths of Mexico City. Isn't this what cyberspace is all about? Once we sat around bonfires. Now we warm ourselves by a flickering computer screen, spreading gossip, catching up on the news.

There was only one problem. I had just recently bought a computer, took a class, and learned the difference between the hard drive and software, downloading and defragmenting, etcetera. As beginners, though, we never touched on how to browse the World Wide Web.

Undaunted by my ignorance, I signed on and began clicking my way into wonderland. My mouse scampered toward a sign that said "Spanish Family." Not exactly Pablo Neruda's *The Heights of Machu Picchu,* I thought, but you've got to start somewhere. Maybe I'd hit on a Júarez station where I could listen to the news and upgrade my Spanish.

Nothing is simple anymore. Next thing I knew, my screen reconfigured itself into an illuminated manuscript of sorts. A caucasian Jesus, Mary, and Joseph appeared before me, glowing. Arrows indicated choices, too many. I could click on the creed, the Our Father, or a Hail Mary.

I clicked. A voice came forth. It spoke Spanish and proceeded to instruct me in the finer points of the mysteries of the holy rosary.

The recitation began. The voice recited the first half of the Hail Mary. A group chimed in on the final Santa María, Madre de Dios, ruega por nosotros pecadores, ahora y en la hora de nuestra muerte, amen.

I pulled my hands back from the keys. Should I close my eyes? Should I pray along? Should I call AOL and tell them off? I examined my motives. As usual, they were mixed.

I could pray the rosary, offering it up for my friends and their various ailments, an undertaking I believe should be central to Catholic spiritual practice.

Or I could bypass God altogether and recite the rosary the way one downs a shot of tequila: for the sheer pleasure of it, for the linguistic rush of reciting what I've long ago memorized but that tastes better each time it touches the tongue.

Nothing in the catechism prepared me for this, I thought, appreciating how new technology must throw every generation's doctrines for a loop. My grandma's ancient *St. Joseph's Daily Missal* made it clear that she could say the rosary while driving. Even if she didn't have beads in hand, she could still deduct days from purgatory so long as the beads were inside the car.

I figured I should probably go to my bedroom and get my mother's first communion rosary, which I keep by my bed. I looked at the clock on my computer. The hour was late. Suddenly my motives became pure as light. I wanted out. I wanted to put on my pajamas and go straight to sleep.

I pointed, clicked, and closed repeatedly until, mercifully, my e-mail screen reappeared.

But the voice was still there. It was like something out of a horror movie. The rosary continued to recite itself.

For ten minutes I pressed buttons, fearful that the computer was on the verge of a breakdown. I was getting anxious if not sick. I remembered to breathe. I shut the thing down.

AOL put me on hold for fifteen minutes.

"Either we are witnessing a miracle," I announced, "or else I mucked things up badly."

"I'm not sure what you did," the man said. "But that was no radio station. It's a program that you downloaded. You can toss it in your computer's trashcan."

Nothing in the catechism had prepared me for that one either. It was the rosary, after all. I remembered the uproar with the advent of televised masses. Did it cheapen the meaning of mass? Did it fulfill Sunday obligation?

The line of questioning still holds. Can mystery light up our lives if it has to pass first through a screen—television or computer?

I'll leave these ponderings to the theologians. For now, I'll play it safe and savor the greatest mystery of them all: That I can stick a message in a bottle and toss it into the great cybersea, and somewhere near or far, a friend will receive it and respond.

Thank heavens for e-mail. ▪

2001

Left Behind

Road rage is so passé. Ditto, going postal. If I'm going in for the kill, I want to shoot up somebody on the other end of the telephone line. Except that there is no one there.

"Please listen carefully as the menu has changed," says a computer. "Select 'one' if this involves a billing question. Select 'two' if you want to hear about our free upgrades. Select 'three' if you—" I sense my life ticking away until at last, my number comes up. I make my selection, but what follows is a cascade of more menu options when all I desire is a human being, a la carte, who can tell me how to revive my computer monitor.

Frantic, I hit zero, an old trick for targeting a human being.

"I'm sorry," says the voice. "Please hang up and try again."

So this is what the Rapture will be like. Maybe it has already happened. Earlier in the day, I'd gone to my local computer service center. It was dark, locked up. A sign said it had closed for good. Gone was the young woman in the polo shirt and gold cross who had always delivered the results of my machine's biopsy, and the bill, with a smile.

So I called the company's 1-800 number: the 666 in an antichrist world devoid of the human touch.

The second time around, I get a nice enough kid named Chris. He walks me through the steps and determines my monitor has died for good. He helps me order a new one. He sounds like he's far away, in Biloxi or Bombay maybe. My heart rate slows down. How can I be angry at him? It won't be long before his job is outsourced to Mars.

If this is the Rapture, then I am left behind. I yearn for the days when we had fewer menu options, fewer options period. Back then you met the people who actually fixed your things—when things could still be fixed. Those days are not likely to return.

Better to resign myself to spending a lot of my life on hold. The desk where I answer my phone could easily be transformed into a little altar—with spiritual reading, incense, etcetera—to remind me of the spiritual truth that linear time is a human construct. We imagine we can multitask our way to nirvana. But time is not ours to save. With God's grace, however, we can learn to savor it—even if we have to hang up and try again.   ▪

2004

Critical Mass

It's official: Latinos are now the largest minority in the United States. At 37 million we have exceeded the numbers of African Americans, according to Census Bureau data released in January.

How will the white majority of U.S. citizens digest the news? Only two weeks before the bureau published the data, a white woman in Phoenix looked me straight in the eye as she picked at her lettuce, which was served to her by a Latino (and no doubt picked by one), and said, "It's turning into Mexico here."

Not all racism is so blatant. It takes the form of intellectual sloth among the media's talking heads who, when talking race, can't think outside of the black-and-white box.

This is true among leftists. As I've written before, the most significant books and documentaries about the 1960s largely ignore the Chicano movement, and Latino activism against the Vietnam War. (See Elizabeth Martínez's analysis in *De Colores Means All of Us: Latina Views for a Multi-Colored Century.*) White intellectuals who should know better are hard pressed to name a dozen of the top Latino intellectuals in this country.

And in progressive church circles, tokenism remains rife. It is easy enough to squeeze Latino concerns onto agendas, or to scare up a Latino to give a workshop at a church conference. It is something else altogether to set agendas aside and to get to know us—from university professors to undocumented workers—as equals.

My state of the union spiel on white–brown relations is not all bleak, however. One of the most heartening things we're witnessing today is the growing numbers of non-Latinos who want to learn to speak Spanish, and who are urging their children to do so. I'm often asked what is the best way to go about learning Spanish, or to improve one's skills. My advice: Total immersion begins at home. Every year countless folks pack their Birkenstocks and set out for Guatemala to study the language in earnest. They come back and all too often lose it because they don't use it. Still others talk wistfully of making such a pilgrimage; meanwhile they spend a small fortune on books and tapes—but can't get it together to drive across town (or walk down the street) to attend Spanish Mass.

I bring up Spanish Mass because, for Catholics, the liturgy offers a perfect way to tune the ear and untwist the tongue. We are already intimate with the cadences and content of the English-language Mass. We've heard it all a million times before, and a million times the words have soothed and renewed. In such an ambience the mind translates, almost organically, from Spanish to English and back again. Introduce music, and whole new regions of the brain light up.

Parish task forces or grassroots organizations that conduct their affairs in Spanish offer other venues for learning. The student of Spanish, perhaps not yet prepared to speak, should sit back and listen in silence for months if need be—not only to words but also beyond words to the very music of communication. One does not acquire a language like a wardrobe. Instead, we must be present to others, humbly open to learning from the "strangers" among us.

So much of learning another language is about relinquishing power and being okay with feelings of fear or embarrassment. English speakers, Hispanics included, can be shamefully oblivious to the power we wield, how we control the discourse among those whose English is less than perfect, or who speak with an accent. The true student is willing to walk in another person's huaraches.

And what a walk! The labyrinth of language, after all, leads back in time, straight to the heart of a culture. The word "ojalá," for example, means "I hope so," or "hopefully." Ojalá has its roots in Moorish Spain; you can hear the echo of the word "allah." To hope is to hope in God.

Many Latinos, even the agnostics and monolingual English speakers among us, pepper conversations with the name of God. We could be talking about the price of gasoline. We catch ourselves sounding just like our grandmothers: "God willing." "Thanks be to God." On television the other night, a Saudi Arabian prince speculating on the war said, "God only knows." This expression, quirky yet reverent, is one I hope never goes extinct.

Learning another language is more than a linguistic endeavor. It is a spiritual one. Word by word, we fall in love not so much with a vocabulary but with a people. If we become fluent, fine. If not, that's fine too. It's the expression of solidarity that counts, the word made flesh in our yearning to connect. ■

2003

Body and Blood

In the course of my travels, I was invited to a Saturday night Mass. Over thirty people squeezed into the living room of a private home, a cozy setup of sofas and lawn chairs, wheelchair and piano bench. Strangely enough, the faithful faced not a makeshift altar but a television set. I figured this must be a special occasion. Maybe we'd see a famous bishop, or the pope even, do his thing on the big screen.

I was wrong. Before Mass got under way, we viewed a twenty-minute video about the School of the Americas in Fort Benning, Georgia, called *SOA: Guns and Greed*. The film, produced by the Maryknolls, documents the links between the school's graduates and the repression of popular movements for justice in Latin America. Trained by the U.S. military, which claims it teaches human rights, graduates have gone on to kill, torture, and disappear people. The film showed how school graduates and their associates had been involved in the martyrdom of many Salvadorans, including Archbishop Oscar Romero.

The film angered and saddened us, yet also gave us reason to hope. Determination to close the school has galvanized activists from around the world. We saw faces, joyful and prayerful, young and old, who have protested in Fort Benning, Georgia, many risking arrest. It's a movement that is growing.

The film ended. The television was set off to the side. In its place sat the priest and the couple in whose house we met.

The Mass proceeded in all its glory. When it was time for the gospel, we heard the story of the widow's mite. In place of a sermon, people offered inspired thoughts, Quaker style. Many praised the generosity of the poor widow. She had given far more than she could afford. One man had a different take—that woman needed every last cent for herself. The point of the story is not so much to glorify her act, he said, but to condemn the powerful who cough up so little, those people whose stake in the status quo keep such women downtrodden in the first place.

We moved on. Prayers from my childhood sweetened my lips. Pita bread was blessed and broken, the wine poured. The basket of bread traveled from hand to hand. The chalice followed. Songs wafted up from the people and a tape player. Thoughts of God filled our heads.

Then—don't ask me what provoked it—I suffered what can only be described, God forgive me, as a Ratzinger moment.

Cardinal Joseph Ratzinger, head of the Vatican's Sacred Congregation for the Faith (formerly the Office of the Inquisition), has made his career by attempting to squash progressive movements for reform in our church, in the United States, and abroad.

I looked around at our group and wondered what he would think. Was it not a priest and two women who poured the wine and divided the pita? Didn't they also, together, utter the pertinent prayers? Surely Ratzinger would cry foul: The laity did not line up for communion; instead our ordinary hands had passed around the bread and wine. We whispered "body of Christ" and "blood of Christ" to one another.

To make matters worse, a daughter of refugees had said a prayer reserved for a male cleric. And the word "Father" to refer to God—I don't think I'd heard it even once. The beautifully written and photocopied liturgy had been authored by women who used gender-neutral names to speak of the almighty.

I tried to quiet my mind. The chalice was still working its way toward me. I scanned the faces of the faithful. No doubt an anonymous exit poll would reveal that members of other Christian denominations lurked among us.

Father Rick (name changed to protect us all) asked those heading to Fort Benning to stand up. About a dozen did so. These good souls soon would join thousands for the annual

November demonstration calling for the closing of the School of the Americas.

Father Rick sprinkled them with holy water. He said a blessing. I felt a drop on my forehead. I flashed back to the film we'd seen: the suffering of Central America, Christ's blood poured out on sidewalks and roadblocks, his body broken by death squads in parish halls and union halls.

And I saw Christ rising—in the lives of babies being pushed around in strollers by parents and grandparents at the Fort Benning protest, in solidarity with activists throughout Latin America.

My Ratzinger moment evaporated. My heart and arms felt strong, the way they should feel when we desire to do the work of rolling away the stone, when Mass has ended and we go in peace, to love and serve our God. ∎

2001

Down There

One of tens of thousands of Bosnian women who were raped in the 1990s speaks of her vagina as a village that has been butchered and burned down: "I do not touch now. Do not visit. I live someplace else now. I don't know where that is."

You'd think Catholic colleges would feel a moral obligation to hear this and other women's testimonies about the sundering of body and spirit so magnificently rendered in *The Vagina Monologues,* by Eve Ensler. But no. The play—the focus of an international movement to end violence against girls and women—has been denied approval or cancelled at more than a dozen Catholic university campuses in February and March of this year.

Some Catholic administrators are calling the monologues "vulgar" and "offensive to women." You could say that about parts of the Bible, but that doesn't take away from the larger narrative, which has revolutionized lives. And this is precisely what the monologues are doing for so many women today.

The play, based on two hundred interviews, contemplates not only the horrors of violence but also what can bring healing: birthing, sex, humor about one's body, and talking, at long last, about past hurts. "You got an old lady to talk about her down there," says one woman, after recounting how she had feared and despised her younger female self. "You know, actually, you're the first person I ever talked to about this, and I feel a little better."

The Vagina Monologues is more than a play. It's a miracle. I saw the first U.S. Spanish-language production of it in Tucson a few years ago, starring local actresses as well as women who'd never stood on a stage in their lives.

Almost five hundred mostly Chicana and Mexican women, old and young, packed a community center. An African friend who had undergone genital mutilation was present, as were a respectable number of men. As with any gathering of women, most participants either knew someone who'd suffered sexual assault or had themselves suffered such a nightmare.

Each monologue took us on a journey "down there" to the site of so much pain, shame, and pleasure.

The audience laughed, wept, flinched with embarrassment, then exhaled with relief. We looked around with pride. Most of us had been brought up Catholic, a condition that despite church theory had not done much to integrate our spirits with our lived physical realities. Storytelling—*The Vagina Monologues*—provided the necessary ceremony. And proceeds from the play benefited a local women's shelter. The monologues have also helped launch the first rape crisis center in the former Yugoslavia and provided aid to clandestine schools for Afghan women.

In the introduction to the book *The Vagina Monologues,* Ensler writes,

> It dawned on me that nothing was more important than stopping violence toward women—that the desecration of women indicated the failure of human beings to honor and protect life and that this failing would, if we did not correct it, be the end of us all. I do not think I am being extreme. When you rape, beat, maim, mutilate, burn, bury and terrorize women, you destroy the essential life energy on the planet. You force what is meant to be open, trusting, nurturing, creative, and alive to be bent, infertile, and broken.

I congratulate the young Catholic women and their allies who are struggling to produce *The Vagina Monologues.* And congratulations to the colleges where it has been shown. What you stand for could well save the world. And maybe even the church. ▪

2004

In Loving Memory

Recently my tía Consuelo passed away, my great-aunt who, as a child, performed with her sister and father in the carpas, the tent circuses of Mexico. I didn't know her as well as I knew her sister, Tía Elvira, who gave me a thick notebook of skits and poems her father wrote for their performances. Tía Elvira and I shared a passion for traditional remedios. She kept fish eyes in her freezer—I was so taken by the sight, I forgot what she prescribed them for.

She also kept herbs in her shed. Some of these she had purchased "over there," she said, pointing south with chin and pursed lips toward a neighbor's house. That was how she referred to Mexico. I half expected to turn around and see Júarez looming through the window of her home in Albuquerque's south valley.

Most branches of my family are rooted, thanks to land grants, in the New Mexico soil, dating back hundreds of years. My tías, however, were born in California and raised in Mexico. And their half sister, my grandma María de Jesus, was born in Mexico, then brought up in the Southwest. Grandma often took a day-long bus ride to Mexico for church meetings; like her siblings, she drew a borderless map in my mind in which Mexico abutted Albuquerque.

I went to the wake at St. Anne's Catholic Church to pay my respects to my tía Consuelo, and—having relocated to New Mexico after a decade—to reconnect with family members. I introduced myself to distant relatives. "Yo soy la hija de Teodoro y Dolores." Two women approached me, all smiles. "Did you say you were the daughter of Ted? We're Lela and Lola. Our mother was Ofelia, the sister of your grandpa Luis, who was our uncle!"

I've come to live for such moments, which are frequent in New Mexico: Someone tosses out a name, and we connect the dots. Second cousin? Third cousin? Something else altogether? At a reading a woman came up to me and said, "My grandpa was Esequiel. He would have been, let's see, the brother of your father's father, my great-uncle." I joyfully signed her book as I did the math in my head. There's nothing in the world quite like the geometry of clan.

I entered St. Anne's Catholic Church with my cousin Cecile. So many of our elders have died that it falls to us, the next generation, to make the round of rosaries, to help reweave the web of family. We embraced our great-uncle. We approached our aunt's coffin and whispered our farewells.

"She looks just like she's asleep," I said, reaching for the nearest cliché to stem my sorrow. I wondered about her life, the stories told but especially those untold. The passing of an elder is like the destruction of a wing of the Smithsonian. Some things remain depressingly irretrievable.

Mercifully, tears and mirth often team up at religious affairs. Tía Consuelo did not disappoint.

We took our place in the pews. I gazed down at my aunt's holy card, which bore a beautiful image of a dark brown Virgen de Guadalupe, de facto goddess of Mexico, much as the church hierarchy won't hear of it.

I flipped the card over. The prayer for the dearly deceased read: "May the Angles lead you into Paradise, may the Martyrs receive you. . . . May the choirs of Angles receive you and may you with the once poor Lazarus, have rest everlasting." I elbowed my cousin and pointed out the mortuary's typo. We bowed our heads. There is no laughter as sweet as that which one must swallow inside a church.

"At least it didn't say choirs of Anglos," my sister later observed.

Anglos, angles, angels: by whatever name, a diverse crowd will greet my tía. Grandma María de Jesus belonged to a Spanish Assemblies of God church. Tía Elvira was a Mormon. My great-grandpa Trinidad was a founding member of a Presbyterian church. They anticipated the dispersal we see today as Latinos leave the church for other faiths—even as we make up nearly 40 percent of the Catholic population. We are not the church's "children," and when the church—from hierarchy to rank and file—treats us as such, we walk.

By all accounts, my aunt loved her faith. She received communion not long before she died. Thankfully, our Mexican heritage teaches us to revere, not fear death. For this reason, toward the end of October, many of us construct elaborate altars for el Día de los Muertos, the Day of the Dead.

This practice has grown in New Mexico, in large part because of the influx of Mexican immigrants. Around Albuquerque, candles burn before photos of relatives who've passed on. Artists and activists place candy before images of Frida Kahlo and Emiliano Zapata. A class in the University of New Mexico's Spanish and Portuguese Department is honoring the countless women maquiladora workers of Júarez who have been murdered in a still unsolved mystery.

So here's to you, in loving memory: Tía Consuelo, Senator Paul Wellstone, and poet June Jordan. Wherever you are, welcome home. ∎

2002

Leaps of Faith

Throughout the ages human beings have opened up the Bible and seen reasons to keep slaves, deny that Native peoples and blacks have souls, burn Jews at the stake, stone women, kill innocent civilians to advance national interests, deny women access to birth control—the list goes on and on.

Yet through it all, God has raised up individuals who have rescued the Word from those whose strange interpretations advance cruelty and injustice. Lovingly and prayerfully, often at great risk to their careers if not their lives, they revisit the scriptures and let God reveal him- or herself anew. Thanks to them, we read the same Bible as the slaveholder did, but we no longer believe that God is for slavery.

God cannot be contained by human stupidity and prejudice; I therefore have no doubt that the Catholic Church will one day welcome to the altar gays who wish to marry. Until then, I propose that Catholics everywhere dust off their rosaries and set aside time each day or week for prayer on behalf of theologians and others engaged in the scholarship that will allow God, once again, to enlighten us, to liberate us from our prejudices, this time as regards homosexuality. Making our views known to the church hierarchy is not enough: The church is no democracy; what we need is a miracle. And this requires prayer—in the name of our gay brothers and sisters wounded by hatred; in the name of those slain at the hands of governments, clerics, and fellow citizens; and in memory of the homosexuals who perished in Hitler's death camps.

Most laypeople will welcome a formal doctrine in support of gay marriage; the rest will catch up. Laypeople tend to be ahead of the game. We are not, for the most part, celibate men; we have different ideas from the church hierarchy, rooted in experience, about the sacredness of desire. From the use of birth control to loving support extended to gay children, ordinary Catholics honor God by respecting reality, by shedding images that demean God. We do not sit around imagining God in heaven sick at heart about a slow procreation day or prayers said by a lesbian couple at Thanksgiving dinner.

Many years ago I read a message that was printed on a bumper sticker or T-shirt that went something like this: "If a man kills another man he is a hero. If he loves another man he is evil." It brings to mind a press conference (before the U.S. invasion of Iraq) in which George W. Bush said that he was at peace with the prospect of war. "I read my Bible every day," he said. Truly our civilization is threatened, not by love and marriage, as our president would have us believe, but by the right-wing hijacking of the religious imagination. The president's Jesus hates gay love and condones warfare and its fallout: death, maiming, environmental catastrophe, devastated minds, massive deficits, and the slashing of basic social services that are the mark of a humane society.

Religious concerns aside, the issue of public policy in a pluralistic society must be dealt with. If heterosexuals don't want to share the word "marriage" with gays, so be it. Extend to those who enter into "civil unions" the same one thousand-plus government-bestowed benefits, responsibilities, and privileges that married couples automatically receive.

Heterosexuals who think gay couples are undermining their marriages should seek help, because nearly half of all heterosexual marriages end in divorce. (This was true long before same-sex marriage became a national issue.) The state should make free counseling available to households headed by heterosexual couples, given the historical tendency of such families to be the site of infidelity and violence against women and children.

Finally, the Catholic Church should immediately suspend use of the word "disordered" to describe homosexuality and turn its energies to addressing the disorders that plague heterosexual marriages. ■

2004

Road Tripping

I was feeling high after a road trip to Clovis, New Mexico, where, flush with spring, I bought a six-hundred-dollar pair of cowboy boots for one hundred and fifty dollars. "I think it's time for me to date again," I told my friend Sharon, as we drove in the dark back to Albuquerque. "Help me compose a personal ad."

"Ivy League–educated Latina Catholic female, forty-three, divorced, seeks brilliant conversationalist," I said, as Sharon popped *Buddy Holly's Greatest Hits* into her CD player. "Or how's this? 'Irreverent forty-three-year-old Catholic news junkie, semivegetarian, seeks brilliant conversationalist.'"

Holly crooned "Peggy Sue, Peggy Sue." I was on a roll. "Fan of John Kerry, Amy Goodman, and Mariachi Masses, forty-three, seeks brilliant—" Sharon broke in. "Serial killers are brilliant conversationalists," she said. "You'd better be more specific about what you want in a partner. Besides, you've had far better luck with Jews than Catholics."

Sharon, a Jew whose partner of twelve years is a WASP, had a point. Today Catholics in the United States meet and mate across religious and cultural borders, and no Catholic believer in his or her right mind, thanks largely to Vatican II, fears hellfire for it.

"Yeah, but I'm not ready to throw in the towel," I said. "I'll happily go out with a Catholic."

I explained. We could go to Mass together. We could shore up one another's faith in the wake of the priest pedophilia scandal. We'd serve soup at the local Catholic Worker house. "And surely a progressive priest out there would show me some loopholes in the annulment process. I've heard it's been done."

"Besides, everybody's going Buddhist," I said. "My new love and I could wrap rosaries around our wrists and meditate. Start a trend maybe. Sell them at the flea market and subsidize our voluntary poverty."

The lights of Albuquerque glittered up ahead when Sharon declared, "Religion. Politics. You're missing the whole point! You want someone who will savor life's little pleasures with you. Someone, maybe even a Republican, who will drive with you to little New Mexico towns to see the sights. Put that in the ad."

"I don't know, Sharon," I said. "This whole thing is turning into a full-blown identity crisis."

"No problema," she said. "Just run three ads highlighting different aspects of your identity and trust the universe."

"But I contain multitudes," I said.

She was not deterred: "Here's a word for you. 'Bashert.' It's Yiddish for 'meant to be.' Whoever is meant to be will be yours."

"Oy vey," I moan. "God willing, it'll also be someone who loves to cook." ▪

2004

Appeal from a Pro-choice Catholic

Today we are witnessing the opening up of political space in what has been the subject of a hopelessly polarized debate, namely abortion. This, thanks to the vision of the Seamless Garment Network. The organization opposes not only abortion but also the death penalty, the arms race, and other threats to life's sanctity.

What makes the Seamless Garment Network unique, however, is that it is a coalition of activists who agree to disagree on whether to criminalize abortion—and who therefore champion a more inclusive and, I believe, revolutionary cause.

The network's goal is not to expend its resources trying to make abortion illegal. Its goal is to "make abortion unthinkable," according to the network's executive director, Mary Rider.

It's an idea whose time has come. The network must seize the moment to reach out to people who have grown numb to the predictable discourse of both pro-life and pro-choice advocates, to win their trust by showing that people on both sides of the issue can work together.

I am convinced that the pro-life movement has not been ambitious enough. Pro-life activists have largely failed to analyze and to publicize various forms of violence perpetrated against the unborn.

Take the epidemic of domestic violence as an example.

What if activists loudly and consistently spoke out for the millions of women whose desires for healthy pregnancies are thwarted by violence—violence that takes place not at abortion clinics but in the so-called sanctity of the home? Where the deadly weapon is not an abortionist's syringe but the fist of a man who claims to love the woman he's beating up.

There's a new study out on women's health titled, "Ending Violence Against Women." It was released by Johns Hopkins School of Public Health and the Center for Health and Gender Equity. One of every three women worldwide has been beaten, raped, or somehow mistreated, according to the report. Besides immediate physical injuries, such treatment of women has been linked to problem pregnancies. The report states that studies have linked abuse of women to miscarriages, premature labor, and fetal distress.

This global perspective reflects what we know about the United States in particular: Violence against women is as American as apple pie. In this country, domestic violence is the leading cause of injury to women. The Justice Department estimates that each year 3 to 4 million women are beaten in their homes.

According to the Centers for Disease Control and Prevention, three-quarters of women over the age of eighteen who are raped or assaulted are victimized by husbands or ex-husbands, boyfriends or ex-boyfriends, the person they live with or a date.

Pregnant women and those who don't yet know they are pregnant pay a heavy price, according to Lorena Howard. "It happens all the time. Women have told me about losing two or more babies because they were beaten," she said. A leading Chicana activist in Tucson, Arizona, Howard works at a shelter for battered women.

Problem pregnancies are often made worse when women smoke and drink because of the stress of "living under siege," she said.

She recently visited with a woman at a Catholic hospital— thirty-five weeks' pregnant—whose partner had punched her in the stomach.

"Think of it," said Howard. "It's living at war."

Making domestic violence a pro-life issue would go a long way toward saving unborn children—and their mothers, she said. (In 1998, almost a third of women murdered in this country were killed by husbands, ex-husbands, boyfriends, or ex-boyfriends, according to FBI statistics.) Perhaps churches could declare themselves sanctuaries for battered women.

Such a campaign would also require taking a hard look at how we can better socialize boys and rehabilitate male abusers, how we can confront the myth that violent behavior is part of proving one's manhood or an appropriate way to vent anger.

Then of course there is the problem of state violence against women and the unborn: the refusal, on the part of the richest nation in the world, to meet the basic needs of its poorest citizens.

Our economy may be prospering, but millions of women are not.

They lack the basics that facilitate a healthy pregnancy, such as health insurance, good food, and an environment free of toxins linked to miscarriages and so on. This situation will persist as long as politicians continue to pat babies on the head with one hand and throw money at the Pentagon with the other.

The antiabortion movement, like all social movements, has relied heavily on political theater: praying the rosary in silence in front of clinics, crying out to women not to kill their babies, or demonstrating with blowup photographs of fetuses.

The challenge for the Seamless Garment Network is to come up with potent symbols that can galvanize a new generation of activists. Why not march with photos of fetuses to the offices of politicians who refuse to support universal health care? Or pray the rosary in the lobby of the senator who axes funding for battered women's shelters, job training, and day care—programs that would reduce women's economic dependency upon their abusers?

Why not march on the Pentagon and run a full-page ad in the *New York Times* on defense spending titled, "Who Are the Real Baby Killers?"

The list goes on. The Seamless Garment Network has won half the battle, by finding some common ground that people on both sides of the abortion issue can stand on. The group offers hope for changing the terms of the debate. A lot of people will be watching. ▪

2000

The Word and the Sword

"Forget about hesitating," says Bob, my instructor in Kendo, the Japanese art of sword fighting. "Abandon all fear." We grip our shinais, swords made of bamboo. Standing about six feet apart, we point the tips of our swords at each other's throats.

Bob wants me to charge, to go for his head, which is caged in a mask called a "men." We are not samurais. We are not fighting to the death. The strikes that we practice—blows to the head, the wrist (kote), and the torso (do)—are but elegant brush strokes, mere signatures of ancient Japanese warrior arts.

"But you've got the experience," I tell Bob. "You're going to get to me first."

My padded hands squeeze the sword even harder. I command them to arc upward but nothing happens. Earlier today my hands went rigid when they were supposed to be moving a pencil across a page. My demon: If I can't be perfect, I don't want to do it. Perfectionism affects even my spiritual life. If I lack the faith others seem to have, prayers die in my throat. In dismay I peer at my teacher through the bars of my mask. He has conjured all my shadows. Which is what Kendo should do given that it is an art, not a sport.

I want Bob to offer me technical advice, but he won't do it; he's on to me. Instead he tells me, "Abandon all hope."

The right words at the right time can act upon the universe like a prayer of exorcism. The core of my being softens. I push off with my left foot, which is barely visible beneath my sweeping blue hakama. My body, though it bears the weight of my armor, is in flight. Too late, Bob's sword reaches my men first. The metal sings. But so what? My very cells are dancing. This is how it feels to abandon all hope.

Bob has me repeat the motion again and again. Each time he shows me how to do it better. "Hold the center," he says. The tip mustn't veer even an eighth of an inch off its trajectory. A practitioner of Kendo devotes endless, often frustrating hours over a lifetime to such drills—all for a few minutes of keiko, or combat, when we see if what we've learned has migrated from our minds to our muscles. The idea is to keep from giving an opponent an opening. One or two times I manage a clean blow.

I take a vow. Each time I sit down to write, or to pray, I will abandon all hope. I will push forward with my pencil, or my mantra, flying and falling and flying again. I will worry less about what I am trying to say and pay more attention to what the practice of writing is saying to me. I will worry less about the strength of my belief in God and rest in the knowledge that it is enough that s/he believes in me. ▪

2004

The Opposite Direction

My mom and I—we go back and forth between burial and cremation. The discussion took a new turn when her youngest, Dominic, proposed that the Martínez family and spouses go with cremation, then have our ashes buried in one place.

"Your brother thinks death is a big reunion and we'll all be out barbequing," she says, putting her coffee cup down. "I don't think he quite understands that *we* will be barbequed!" We laugh until we have to pat away the tears. Mom is a hospice volunteer. She believes in talking about these things.

Lately, she has been leaning toward burial. Better that the children and grandchildren view her body and come to grips with the fact of her passing on.

"Besides," she says. "I heard that what doesn't burn up, they grind down. Imagine."

"And that's any worse than maggots crawling out of your eyes?" I ask.

Times have changed. A mere one hundred years ago, my mother's grandmother Juanita would line coffins with scraps of cloth for family or neighbors on the occasion of a death. The velorio took place in people's houses. Later everybody met again to return the body to its home under the fertile earth. God's little creatures took care of the rest.

Mom and I poll Dad about cremation; he is not sure what the fuss is about. He is a retired lieutenant colonel in the Marine Corps reserves; all he knows is he has a free plot waiting for him in Santa Fe, the state capitol, if we so choose to put him there.

"The cemetery is visible from the highway," he says breezily. "You can wave to me whenever you're driving north out of town." He reminds me that he wants mariachis at his Mass.

My sister, Elena, will not humor us with an opinion. She thinks my mother and I are morbid.

The idea of Dad ending up in Santa Fe does not sit well with me. I want my family within a stone's throw of one another.

Last year on Christmas Eve, I went for the first time to visit the graves of relatives at the old Albuquerque cemetery. My cousin Cecile invited me. Every year she assembles luminarias, filling brown paper sacks with sand and a votive candle, which she then lights and places near each headstone. Luminarias evolved out of an ancient tradition of bonfires that marked the days leading up to Christmas and that symbolized lighting the way for the Christ child.

"Hi, Grandpa!" said Cecile, gently setting a bag down on the ground next to the tombstone. I reached in and lit the candle. We set down some more bags, her daughter, son, and husband all pitching in. At each relative's grave, my cousin recalled a story I had either forgotten or had not heard.

Everywhere people were setting up luminarias and arranging flowers. Children chased each other. Old people paid their respects then sat down in lawn chairs and enjoyed a picnic lunch. There was music and even some video cameras. My cousin came upon some old friends. This was the place to be if you had gotten lazy about reading the obits and were not sure who had died and who had survived the year.

We left while it was still light, but it was not hard to imagine how beautiful the cemetery would be after nightfall, candles blazing gold through the brown paper.

When I got home, I reported to mom all I had seen. She was impressed that I was impressed; visiting the graves of dead people always struck her as slightly ridiculous.

My five-year-old niece, Rachel, is too young to understand any of this—or so I thought until a few weeks ago. She pressed my mother for details about dying. Mom explained in the simplest terms about physical functions, such as how breathing ends.

Later, Rachel offered her own little insight into death: "It's like borning except the opposite," she announced, out of the blue. "The opposite?" Mom asked. "Yeah. The opposite direction," Rachel answered. ■

2002

Columnas Fronteras

Inherit the Earth

A Moment in History

My spirit moved from New Mexico to Arizona years before the rest of me followed; to be precise, I took up residence in the upper room of Jesus Is Lord Used Tires in Tucson, an establishment created by Barbara Kingsolver in her book *The Bean Trees*. I lived there with Mattie, a big-hearted character who shelters political refugees from Guatemala.

It was an ideal arrangement. The move cost me nothing except seventy-five-cent cups of coffee at Catalina's restaurant in Old Town, the Albuquerque plaza my forebears helped build during the 1700s. There, outdoors on a sun-baked banco, I read for hours, unfazed by San Felipe Church bells dutifully marking the passage of time.

Now and again I glanced up and eyed the small adobe house across the way. I almost forgot. I lived there. Halfway between San Felipe Church and the High Noon Saloon. A few miles from Martíneztown, the barrio that once was my family's land grant from the king of Spain.

I was a New Mexican, a manita, as we're known. I could chatter on, as if it happened yesterday, about an ancestor charged by the Office of the Inquisition with trafficking in "magic roots." I hired genealogists, not astrologists, and my charts divined a web of relations, including Pueblo peoples, the Navajos, and Jews who practiced their faith in secret in New Spain.

Magic roots? You bet. People like me don't pledge allegiance to other states, Jesus Is Lord Used Tires or no.

Fast-forward a year or so to 1989.

I am reading from my poetry at Southside Presbyterian Church in Tucson. In the early 1980s, the church, defying U.S. immigration officials, declared itself a sanctuary for Central American refugees. In 1985, a number of activists, including Southside's pastor, John Fife, were indicted and ultimately convicted for their work with what came to be known as the Sanctuary Movement.

Eyeing my Southside audience I half expected the heavens to open: convicted felons, unindicted coconspirators, the not guilty but not necessarily innocent, and refugee activists who'd suffered under brutal dictatorships. In short, ordinary people who adamantly refused to look the other way. Holiness pervaded the sanctuary proper, an unassuming building in the shadow of the "A" mountain, in need of a coat of paint.

I fought to keep my emotions in check. I was in my glory, vindicated as I stood before this jury of my peers—people who had done worse things than I had.

In 1986, I accompanied to the U.S.–Mexico border a Lutheran minister who along with others brought two refugees into the United States. A religion reporter at the time, I sniffed a potential story.

The women were pregnant, due to give birth in December. Like the Holy Family, they were fleeing oppression, except that the two women's Egypt was El Salvador, where fourteen families owned most of the land; where right-wing death squads "disappeared" those who dared question the status quo; a dictatorship to which the United States was forking over $1 million a day in the name of fighting communism.

Instead of an article, I ended up writing a poem called "Nativity." I read it at Southside and explained that the poem had been used against me in the course of my own indictment and trial. (The poem's punch line: "In my country we sing of a baby in a manger, finance death squads.")

In 1987, I was accused of conspiracy against the U.S. government, of inducing the entry of so-called illegal aliens and aiding in their transport—federal charges that carried a twenty-five-year prison sentence. The minister faced similar charges.

In 1988, following a two-week trial, a jury declared us not guilty: me, on First Amendment grounds; and the minister, for the reason that the year of our fateful trip, then-governor Toney Anaya had proclaimed New Mexico a sanctuary for Central American refugees.

My invitation to read at Southside came from an activist, Rene Franco, who'd barely escaped death at the hands of the Guatemalan military. He dug around for a key hidden near the entrance of a stately abode in one of the better zip codes in Tucson, where he had arranged for me to stay.

Its owner, I would come to find out, had herself barely escaped death—on an operating table while undergoing brain surgery. (She later stunned surgeons by detailing the uproar that ensued when she momentarily died.) Not long after, her husband left her. Reduced to near poverty—to the point of holding periodic yard sales to pay bills—she nonetheless kept current her membership in the Junior League.

Well-spoken, well-coiffed, and well-connected, schooled in the civil rights movement and later a two-time delegate to the Democratic National Convention, this forty-something mother of four was born to aid and abet. And to get away with it.

I dubbed her home "The House of the Spirits," after the book by Isabel Allende, which I read each night before I fell asleep on a mattress that my new friend had set out for me on the floor.

There was always more room at her inn, which was obscured by a thicket of palo verde, olive, and mesquite trees. Out of nowhere appeared mattresses where refugees, some still bearing marks of torture, could lay their heads. By day black beans bubbled in a bottomless pot. Corn tortillas blistered on the burner. Smoke wafted up like incense to pre-Columbian gods.

I noted that my hostess's linen closets were large enough to hide in. She leaned against her cane and smiled. I put nothing past her. She had no qualms about concealing refugees in her car's back seat, then donning her Susan Sarandon smile at agents who waved her and her sons on past the border checkpoint. Once she even managed to secure a bulletproof vest from a friend in law enforcement for use by a Salvadoran clergyman besieged by death threats.

Junior League indeed.

I listened to her stories as we sat in her living room, where ceiling-high shelves bulged with books about the Holocaust. I looked out a large picture window. The day was dying, the sun bleeding on the horizon. I exhaled for the first time, it felt, since my trial. Innocence? Guilt? No, life. The red-orange sky was a welcome. A welcome home.

I would return to Tucson to live three years later, following a stint on the staff of the National Catholic Reporter in Kansas City, Missouri. During my time in the Midwest, an activist priest I nicknamed Father Clip and Save sent envelopes stuffed with articles about life in Arizona.

These included newsletters of goings-on sponsored by various activist groups. Reviewing them, it occurred to me it would be nearly impossible, as a Tucson resident, to suffer a crisis of meaning. Every night of the week there were potlucks, protests, planning meetings, and presentations: Veterans for Peace, Students Against Sweatshops, the Arizona Border Rights Project, Pueblo Por La Paz: Chiapas Coalition—and for Thanksgiving, a vegetarian potluck featuring two live turkeys as honored guests, sponsored by the Vegetarian Resource Group.

If, as the Jews say, one of our purposes in this life is to help repair the earth, then it is heartening to know that Tucson has ample venues for such an undertaking.

I am a New Mexican. Women like me, who dare to fall in love with another state, can always fall back on the salmon defense: We won't die until we make our way upstream to our place of birth.

Until then, forward all my mail to Jesus Is Lord Used Tires. ∎

2000

Inherit the Earth

The Arizona sun is melting like a pat of butter on the mountain that flanks Tucson's west side. As the day dies away, people are gathering at an outdoor shrine known as El Tiradito, in the heart of downtown's Barrio Historico. For fifty weeks, every Thursday night, we have gathered here for a vigil to remember those who perish as they make their brutal pilgrimage across the U.S.–Mexico border.

The shrine is little more than a ruin of a wall, its pockmarked adobes licked by candlelight. Legends have multiplied around the origins of El Tiradito, which means "the castaway." Stories speak of a love triangle in 1870 gone bad, ending in murder, the body abandoned in the hard dirt.

According to the historical marker, "This is the only shrine in the U.S. dedicated to the soul of a sinner buried in unconsecrated ground."

Unconsecrated ground. Reflecting on those words, I can't help but see our border, la frontera: a militarized zone, a killing field. I think of the fourteen men who died recently in triple-digit heat—abandoned by their smuggler, abandoned by a gluttonous nation that craves cheap labor but detests the laborer.

Too, I think of the hope that guides such men, women, and children north. Only hope, biblical in proportion, would compel Yolanda Gonzales, on Memorial Day of last year, to pour the last drops of water from her plastic jug into her daughter's bottle. The mother died in the Arizona desert. The baby, named Elizama, survived.

To speak of an immigrant's plight only in terms of desperation fails to honor his or her full humanity. Of course there is desperation; everywhere it uproots and drives masses across borders in swelling numbers.

Still, whereas desperation drives people, hope guides them. With a patience that rivals that of Job's, the migrant gathers information, plans, packs, says good-bye to her family, then strikes out. It is not Disneyland she hopes for, but dignity.

Perhaps it is such hope that consecrates the blistering desert terrain where so many have fallen. Even in death, the fourteen Mexican migrants live on as a sign: The forces of militarization and xenophobia will not stop a single determined soul from putting one foot in front of the other, plastic water jug in hand.

At our vigil we hold up a white wooden cross. It is marked with the word "Presente." Yes, the dead live among us, as martyrs, as prophets. Their lives—their hunger and their hope—add up to a cry that will be heard around the globe. A cry for change. A demand that we heal our tortured border, that we reconsecrate the earth. ▪

2001

The Things They Carried

Is it an art installation or an altar? At First Christian Church in Tucson, a museum-quality display case holds, among a number of objects, the following: empty plastic water jugs, a backpack, a baby bottle, soap, Colgate toothpaste, a hairbrush, a sardine can, a sock, and used AeroMéxico tickets.

When Mexican migrants fan out across the treacherous Arizona desert border region, these are some of the things they carry. On foot a person might cover eight to ten miles a day—or fewer miles if carrying a baby. Many try to beat those odds. The exhibit includes a stroller. A Caribou bicycle is also on display, its tire tubes all shot to hell, punctured by cactus needles from the trek through an impossible terrain.

"We find about one hundred bicycles a week," said Reverend Robin Hoover, pastor at First Christian and founder of Humane Borders, which has maintained water stations for migrants, mostly on public lands, in the most desolate areas of Arizona for more than a year. The U.S. Border Patrol has pledged not to target the water stations, and it recently credited the availability of the large barrels of water with saving thirty-three lives in just one day. Many fear the stations will inevitably become a target for agents rounding up Mexicans.

The installation, put together by Maeve Hickey of Dublin, is called Lost and Found: Remnants of a Desert Passage. She selected items from the hundreds that Humane Borders volunteers have collected on their frequent trips to haul water to the stations.

Standing before the glass case, Hoover explained that the Caribou bike was found about twenty-three miles north of the border in Organ Pipe Cactus National Monument.

The stroller was found twenty-one miles north of the U.S.–Mexico border at the Jim Corbett water station in Organ Pipe. Named after the deceased Sanctuary Movement founder, Jim Corbett station has dispensed the most water of all fourteen stations Humane Borders maintains.

"We've even found baby's cowboy boots with silver tips," said Hoover, adding that he doesn't know what fate the owner of the stroller or the babies met.

As to the many personal hygiene items volunteers find at water stations: "Migrants think they've made it, and now they're going to freshen up," Hoover said.

In fact a lot of migrants have no idea where they are in relation to where they want to end up.

Hoover said most have their sights on Florida, the Bay Area, Los Angeles, Chicago, New York, New Jersey, and anywhere in Texas. Depending on where they started along Arizona's almost three-hundred-mile border with Mexico, they press northward: through Organ Pipe Cactus National Monument, Buenos Aires National Wildlife Refuge, Cabeza Prieta National Wildlife Refuge, the Tohono O'odham Indian Reservation, and other, mostly public, lands.

Some groups have arranged ahead of time for rides that they'll meet up with in small towns, or at appointed spots along the highway. Smugglers called "coyotes" guide other groups for a price, often proffering false promise of a nearby city where a ride awaits to take them to their destinations. And still others imagine that Phoenix is just around the bend. They push on.

Volunteers come across many socks. When feet swell, and burrs and needles collect in socks, those are left behind. The most common metal item found, Hoover said, is a poor person's version of a Swiss Army knife, with nail clippers, can opener, and knife. It is used to cut needles out of clothes or the body. People also use the instrument to modify their clothing: to cut off sleeves and shorten pants in triple-digit heat. Another item found: injectable xylocaine to deaden the pain.

The border patrol has, in the past decade, successfully sealed off traditional urban points of entry, such as Júarez–El Paso; hence the large numbers attempting the desert, which in Arizona is mostly under federal, state, tribal, county, or corporate management. The U.S. Fish and Wildlife officials have permitted Humane Borders to erect poles with flags at seven animal watering troughs. The flags bear the symbol of the drinking gourd from the abolitionist movement, with water pouring from the dipper.

Humane Borders provides water to address the immediate emergency, but its ultimate goal is, with other groups, to force changes in U.S. immigration policy—to "take death out of the migration equation," as Hoover puts it.

The length of the entire U.S.–Mexico border is almost two thousand miles; human rights groups estimate that at least one person a day dies trying to cross it.

Remarking on the display, Hoover said he was not sure why someone would carry used AeroMéxico plane tickets, although such documents are often found. Carrying them, an immigrant runs the risk of a border patrol agent using a plane ticket as evidence of country of origin, a basis for deportation. On the other hand, there is an advantage. A name on one's person can help identify remains should one die along the way.

There's much more beyond the large display case of things found in the desert, the things that migrants carry.

At Humane Borders's church office, volunteers have collected a baby's receiving shirt, business cards, a cologne bottle, wedding pictures, crucifixes, a doll, and *Five Minutes of Prayers in the Home,* a Spanish-language booklet dated March 2002.

The desert holds letters lost or left behind. "I love you," reads a handwritten letter in Spanish. "I need you. . . . I hope that very soon we can be together forever." ■

2003

Another Crossing

I'm sitting in bed in a motel, notebook in hand, looking out the window at the ocean. I want to write a poem about the great borderless ocean, the fog, and the shore's edge. But the longer I take in the scenery, the more the scene changes, or maybe it hasn't changed at all, maybe my seeing has: The poetic process forces such shifts. As a result one rarely ends up writing what one intended. Poets set out at times almost arrogantly in search of "material," only to be humbled by another story insisting its way across our borders and onto the page.

SANTA BARBARA, CALIFORNIA

You see them
Everywhere
If you choose:
Hands that push
Rags, rakes, brooms.
And tucked among
The pay stubs,
The Spanish
You forgot
Or never learned.
Tucked among
The soap slivers,
The ceremonies
You forgot
Or never learned.
Soon the maid

Will go home,
Wash her hands,
Make the sign
Of the cross
With an egg
Over the feverish
Body of a child.
You are that child.
The maid, your mother,
Will leave the closet
Light on for you.
When you wake up
You will have the words,
At last, to offer praise. ∎

2003–2004

Driving while Brown

A friend recently remarked, "Remember the good old days when United States citizens could drive freely from city to city?"

We were commiserating about how life for residents of the Southwest has changed. A continually beefed-up U.S. Border Patrol working with the U.S. military has meant that more of us, particularly people of color, are being stopped and searched in the course of our travels within the United States. Not crossing international borders—just driving from point to point inside the country.

My friend, Native American author Leslie Marmon Silko herself has been subject to several random searches in her drives in and around Tucson, Arizona. No matter that she is a winner of both a Pulitzer Prize for fiction and a MacArthur Fellowship. To agents she is just another brown face, another "illegal alien" or potential drug smuggler threatening the American way of life.

The same thing happened to nationally syndicated columnist Roberto Rodriguez, who also happens to be an acclaimed champion of civil and human rights.

In 1979 police clubs rained down on his skull, causing extensive injuries, when he dared to snap pictures of Los Angeles County Sheriff's deputies beating up a young Chicano, Rodney King style. Rodriguez was charged with assaulting officers with a deadly weapon—his camera. Eventually he was cleared of charges, and in 1988 he won a lawsuit against the deputies.

Given his history, Rodriguez was only too happy to cooperate when border patrol agents recently detained him for almost forty-five minutes outside Las Cruces, New Mexico. Rodriguez was driving home to Albuquerque after giving speeches in Los Angeles and Tucson about his new book *Codex Tamuanchan: On Becoming Human,* which explores issues of Chicano identity.

He arrived at the border patrol's Las Cruces checkpoint on I-25 and stated that he is a U.S. citizen. In response to further questioning, Rodriguez explained that he'd been to Los Angeles and Tucson.

At that point, with no explanation, agents initiated a canine search of the car. As dogs sniffed, three agents and two plainclothes officers took apart seats and other car parts. Rodriguez was taken to a nearby office. There, he underwent extensive questioning as to his comings and goings as two armed guards kept watch.

"I felt as if I'd entered the twilight zone," said Rodriguez, recounting the experience. Afterwards, Rodriguez tried to get an explanation for his detention. After a series of nonanswers, Rodriguez said, he decided to file a complaint.

In the past decade, the U.S. Border Patrol has come under fire from groups such as Americas Watch, the American Friends Service Committee, and Amnesty International for abuses by agents and a failure to investigate complaints. Faced with mounting pressure, the patrol has trumpeted its supposed willingness to hear any and all complaints. I talked with Doug Mozier about Rodriguez's situation and others like it; Mozier is the public affairs officer for the agency's El Paso, Texas, sector, which includes New Mexico and parts of West Texas.

Mozier spoke of special hot lines, public forums, and various complaint processes aimed at improving relations between the border patrol and the community. He assured me that the agency welcomes criticism in its effort to improve the way it operates. The spirit of Mozier's comments contrasts starkly, however, with the tone of the response Rodriguez received from Alan Gordon, the acting chief border patrol agent for the sector.

In a letter responding to Rodriguez's complaint, Gordon maintained, among other things, that the border patrol does not "consider it appropriate to express an opinion to persons outside the Immigration and Naturalization Service on legal issues." Gordon goes on to cite various laws that give agents broad discretion when it comes to questioning anybody "about your immigration status and other suspicious circumstances."

The letter lists the following as factors that led to the decision to detain Rodriguez: He'd been traveling a "nondirect route," that is from Los Angeles to Albuquerque via Tucson. Considering that Rodriguez needed to give speeches in Los Angeles and Tucson, and that he lives in Albuquerque, what other route could he have taken?

The letter also alleges that Rodriguez had a "rental" car and that articles such as clothing, toiletries, or foodstuffs—items "consistent with persons in travel"— were nowhere in sight. In fact, Rodriguez had a leased car. And his personal items were in the trunk along with stacks of books. "I plead guilty to a clean car," Rodriguez told me.

After speaking with Mozier, I questioned Ramiro García, a senior border patrol agent who works out of Las Cruces. García allowed that had agents questioned Rodriguez first (before the dogs and detention), they might have learned of the book tour and saved everyone the hassle.

Mistakes are made, García said. Still, "Agents are very experienced in what they do," he said. In the El Paso sector alone (125,000 square miles), more than $190 million worth of narcotics have been nabbed during fiscal year 1999, García said.

Too bad the agency isn't required to do an equally detailed accounting of the numbers of innocent people detained in the name of the drug war. When I asked why agents don't keep such records, Mozier and García said it would be too hard given the volume of traffic moving through the checkpoints.

I find that reasoning hard to swallow. A primitive adding machine could do the trick.

Said Rodriguez: "This isn't even an issue of immigration. I was traveling to nonborder cities. I'm a U.S. citizen."

Rodriguez is also a Latino: offspring of the Spanish conquest, descended from people indigenous to the Americas. And he can't hide his Indian blood. He is as dark as chocolate. For decades, he has written about the irony that those of us who have been on this continent the longest are the ones most likely to be singled out as suspect: Between the drug war and anti-immigrant hysteria, we are viewed as strangers in our own land.

But in his fight for dignity for all people, Rodriguez is not afraid to bear arms. When agents asked Rodriguez if he had any weapons on him, he said, "I carry pens." ∎

1999

Betrayals

I remember the Princeton sweatshirt and the *Wall Street Journal*—or was it Shakespeare's sonnets—that I kept as props in my car when driving north from Mexico after purchasing prescription drugs I couldn't afford in the United States. Approaching the border patrol checkpoint, I slowed down and glanced in the rearview mirror at my chic black glasses as if these, too, could save me.

"Citizenship?" the guard asks, his eyes fixed on my eyes, followed by a hard look at the inside of my car.

"U.S.," I say, my mouth dry with fear. The drugs are in a bag beside me. There is nothing illegal about filling your doctor's prescription in Mexico. Yet each time I do it, I feel like a criminal. When it comes to the U.S. Border Patrol with its props—random checkpoints, fencing made of toxic helicopter landing strips from old U.S. wars, heat-seeking devices, stadium lights, guns, German shepherds, etcetera—terror is the name of the game.

"Have a good day," the guard says. I step on the gas. My lipstick—a deep brown that makes my skin look whiter than it is—feels like wax. Truth is, I can deal with feeling like a criminal. What is harder to acknowledge is feeling like a traitor.

My father's mother, María Jesús, was Mexican by birth, and she looked it: short, with deep brown skin and long hair she put up in a bun or braids, and always dressed modestly in a flowery dress and flat shoes. She had a beautiful, strong Spanish accent. I think of her whenever I make my crossings. The border patrol's mission is to seek out the faces of our Mexican grandmothers, the people who cannot disguise their indigenous features or class origins. They are ordered to special areas, where their vehicles, if not their entire lives, are disassembled. While the citizen-grand-daughters, if we "look American" enough for the authorities, are waved on.

To answer "United States" when asked to name our country of origin forces us to betray our own. For a terrible instant we deny that we are related to the people south of the U.S.–Mexico divide. Borders do that. They cast spells, blinding us to the faces of our own kin. ▪

2004

On Arno Street

Today I want to invite you to go with me back in time to a neighborhood in the soul of Albuquerque. To get there we coast downhill toward the railroad tracks on a one-way street called Lead. Downtown Albuquerque is just ahead, its weary skyline slumbering in the sun. Roll down the window. Listen to the train's sweet moan. I can recall that sound as if I'd heard it yesterday. But in fact it's been almost twenty years since the *Albuquerque Journal* sent a colleague and me one afternoon on a city assignment to find undocumented workers from Mexico. Our editors asked that we interview them and write about their lives. The neighborhood we were headed toward was said to be heavily populated with immigrants. My colleague hung a left on Arno Street and parked the car.

Pens and reporters' notebooks in hand, we locked the car doors then set out, parting ways to cover more ground. This was a poor neighborhood. Many houses were run down, some scarred by boarded windows. Yet they still retained something of their old majesty. Great battered houses, some brick, some Victorian style, two and three stories high, looked like they had been lifted from a fairy tale by a tornado and flung by sheer chance to Albuquerque. No doubt generations of families had sat together on these porches and stoops fanning themselves, telling stories, watching children jump rope and kick balls in the street.

It was on one such cracked stoop that I found Julio.

I introduced myself and asked if I could talk with him. He was more than happy to speak with me on the condition that I change his name. I have discovered, in reporting and in forty-three years of life, that most people want very much to tell their stories, for it is in telling our stories that we emerge from statistics and stereotypes and become human to one another. Julio was no different.

I sat next to him. He stretched his legs out in front of him and took a swig of water from a cracked cup. Like a number of his neighbors, he had recently made the long pilgrimage from Mexico to the United States. He was determined to do anything a United States citizen would not: rip up asphalt in 100-degree heat, balance on ladders and pick oranges in 110-degree heat. No work was beneath him. Quite the opposite. Work, any work, was a gift from God. It gave him dignity, defined him as a man. Work allowed him to survive. What's more, it allowed him to send money to struggling relatives back home in Mexico.

As he spoke, Julio's hands hovered like butterflies with no place to land. Like most Mexican immigrants I knew, Julio dreamed of returning home for good but didn't know if it would be possible, given the economic situation of his country. For now he lived half in the light, half in the shadows: in the light, working whenever the opportunity came up, and in the dark, fearful of being captured and deported by immigration agents. Times were hard, he said with his generous smile, "bien horrible," pretty bad. Still, Julio believed—in opportunity, hard work, and sacrifice on behalf of his family. He believed in the American Dream. He loved the country that wanted his labor but did not want him. He loved and had faith.

We sat together on the stoop like long-lost kin. Come to think of it, we were long-lost kin. We sat in a landscape that not so long ago belonged to Mexico, before the United States seized half of Mexico's landmass. As Chicanos often intone, we did not cross the border—the border crossed us. Julio's pilgrimage north and my pilgrimage south on Arno reunited us as brother and sister.

Julio paused, lost in thought. I looked up at the houses across the street. Sunlight lapped against the brick and stucco and shingle of each home. Curtains fluttered over open kitchen windows; the aromas of onions, garlic, tomatillos, and refried beans took me back to my ancestors' kitchen tables. A woman stepped out on the porch and gathered up her child in her arms. Other mothers leaned out of windows or stood behind torn screen doors. Laundry rippled on lines stretched across dirt yards.

Down the block a man opened the hood of his car and, removing tools from his pocket, started work on repairs. The car, its front doors open, looked like a bird trying to lift off. Music spilled out of the car. Corridos. Norteño. Ranchera. Children appeared out of nowhere, like holy apparitions. Maybe they were coming home from school. Their laughter filled the street. Their faces—brown, white, black—shown like those of little gods.

They were gods, of course, or at least touched by the divine spark. In their innocence, the world belonged to them, a world that they could shape rather than be shaped by—disfigured by—clay they could mold and fire into a new creation. Recent history had birthed movements in which Chicanos, blacks, women, farm workers, Native Americans, and others had dared to take their destinies in their own hands. I looked at the children and wondered, Why not again? Why not social movements demanding schools that nurture children into healthy adults? A livable wage for an honest day's toil? Free medical clinics? Community gardens? Decent, affordable housing for all?

And why not these children, and the Julios of the world, forging the way? No borders had impeded Julio in his journey. Borders had not yet been thrown up around the imaginations of the children. Their migrations, imaginative and actual, forecast a movement beyond the American Dream to a dream of the Américas that excluded no one and no place.

I am not sure now how much time passed as I watched Arno reveal to me its secret life. Half a minute? Half an hour? I can only tell you that time as we know it, the time of clocks and deadlines and daily planners, ceased. And in its place, eternity embraced Arno. A place of so much poverty and displacement became a place of hope, not just for Julio, who knew he'd somehow find work, but for me, who all too easily gave up hope.

Julio wiped the sweat from his brow and ran his hands through his black hair. He smiled, assuring me that if he got deported, he'd be back. I imagined him standing at the Rio Grande. He had no doubts. The Red Sea parted for him.

Before long my colleague appeared in the distance. Soon it would be time to go. With regret I shook Julio's hand and wished him well. Walking toward the car, I smelled the sweet stale perfume of the asphalt. I struggled to memorize the features of each house and tree. I did not want to let this moment go. I feared I would forget. That I would return to the world of statistics and abstractions, justifications and excuses, grand political speeches about poverty, words divorced from the aspirations and stories of real people living on real streets just like this one.

I read piles of newspapers in which opinion makers argue ceaselessly about poverty, war, disease, and the environment. I engage in these debates myself. I have signed petitions, voted, crafted letters to the editor, had bumper stickers made, posted signs in my yard, marched at demonstrations, and took potluck dishes to fundraisers of every sort. But in the uproar, I have often forgotten to be still, forgotten to listen humbly to the Julios of this world.

Listening to the biblical "stranger" among us is a political act, a radical act. Their testimonios spark our imaginations. We sympathize, then we empathize, then we envision a different kind of world, a vision that not only pushes us to action but sustains us in the most difficult of times, when we are tempted to give in to cynicism, numbness, bitterness, fatigue, and hopelessness.

Today we are up against the unthinkable. Environmental catastrophe looms, made worse by war and weapons that are poisoning the earth. At the same time growing numbers of oppressed peoples are determined to heal the earth and to heal themselves. In our poetry and our politics, a new dream is emerging, one that rejects the false dichotomy between nature and the human person, or the citizen and the so-called "stranger."

My great joy as a writer is to explore the inner lives of activists, to bear witness to the ways in which we think globally and act locally—as well as think locally and act globally.

In my novel, *Mother Tongue,* José Luis, the Salvadoran son of my protagonist, grows up to be an environmental activist. Here is what his mother, María, says about him: "Oftentimes, after supper, when I would rather we go on a walk, José Luis descends to the basement where, years ago, we set up his first computer. Messages flash like lightning on the screen and he answers, communicating for hours at a sitting with students in Brazil, biologists in China—wherever wetlands or highlands or any other land is in danger of disappearing, of becoming something it is not due to man-made chemicals that have infiltrated once pristine places . . . How different his universe is from the one Soledad knew. José Luis and his friends cast bottles upon oceans of computer screens, and, in an instant, their messages wash up as far away as Africa. Before history happens—a land takeover, a nuclear waste accident, the death of another species—José Luis knows about it. His is a generation of psychics, not because they can peer into the future but because the sins of earlier generations have forced them to look deeply into the here and now and thereby alter fate. It is a frightful balancing act, attending to the moment in order to create the future. His basement walls are papered with maps of frayed ozone layer, dying forests, dust bowls where crops once thrived. The maps tell the real story of how the world has changed since Soledad was his age. José Luis is caught up in a struggle larger than that of an individual nation. He and his friends talk about saving the planet. I wish I could say they were exaggerating."

Indeed, what a balancing act! Centering ourselves in the here and now to prevent what appears to be inevitable. We need tactics, strategies, campaigns, and movements that embrace the suffering and hope of the entire planet. But we also need the stoop on Arno, where we unshackle our imaginations over and again and become cocreators of our collective reality.

In closing, I'd like to read from the title poem of Martín Espada's book, *Imagine the Angels of Bread.*

If the abolition of slave-manacles
began as a vision of hands without manacles,
then this is the year;

if the shutdown of extermination camps
began as imagination of a land
without barbed wire or the crematorium,
then this is the year;
if every rebellion begins with the idea
that conquerors on horseback
are not many-legged gods, that they too drown
if plunged in the river,
then this is the year.

So may every humiliated mouth,
teeth like desecrated headstones,
fill with the angels of bread.

I urge you to go forward in your work, at once political and sacred, of shattering the spell cast by the powers that be. This, my friends, is the year. ▪

Keynote, Globalization and the Environmental Justice Movement Symposium, Tucson, Arizona, September 23–25, 2004.

La Biblioteca on the Border

The monumental two-story library overlooking the Pacific on the Universidad Iberoamericana campus is the brainchild of Jesuit Father David Ungerleider. A library on a Jesuit campus might not seem unusual, but this is in Tijuana, Mexico, border town, a place of exploitation, violence, and lost dreams.

Yet some, including Ungerleider, assistant to the president of the university, see the city differently, as a place of tremendous artistic and intellectual wealth, full of people wanting to better themselves. That vision dominated the dedication ceremony for the university's new Loyola Library.

"This is history in the making," said novelist Denise Chávez. She was one of several Chicano authors who read from their work on a panel moderated by Mexico's preeminent female author, Elena Poniatovska. Indeed, this is the first time in the history of the Republic of Mexico that a private university has built a library facility for the general public.

"It offers a chance for the people of Tijuana to get ahead in life," said Ungerleider, who has tirelessly accompanied poor people in their struggles since his ordination in 1977.

Ungerleider first dreamed up the idea of a library for the public in 1996. Thanks to benefactors on both sides of the border, including the Lannan Foundation, it is nearing completion. Ungerleider, fifty-two, was born into a family of twelve children (his parents later took in four more children) in upstate New York. After ordination he worked in Philadelphia with Puerto Rican gang members suffering from drug addiction, and he founded a recreation center and later a social service and housing center.

He has spent over twenty years in Mexico. During this time he has taught extensively throughout the country. His degrees include a bachelor's degree in philosophy and letters from St. Louis University and a master's degree in social anthropology from the Escuela Nacional de Antropología e Historia in Mexico City. He teaches once a year at the University of Havana. Ungerleider also spends a week of every month at a hospital he directs, which serves Tarahumara Indians in the Copper Canyon area. And he is constantly raising money for the library.

Three years ago Ungerleider established a mission-style church, built of straw and plaster, for the residents of the colonia near the university; he says Mass there beneath a beautiful white dome that rises up in earthy splendor. The church, La Capilla del Corazón Sagrado, is made of 711 bales of hay, he explained on a tour of the place. The coat of white plaster gives the walls the flowing look of ancient adobe. The rest of the church was put together out of leftovers, rejects, donations, from the altar to the last pew. The stained glass windows, made by a Tijuana artisan, give a "mini-history of salvation for those who cannot read," Ungerleider said.

Ungerleider brought in fiberglass statues of Guadalupe and Joseph from Mexico City. He feared they'd be seized by customs officials at the Tijuana airport. They suspected the priest might be smuggling drugs in the statues. "They looked up St. Joseph's nose for drugs," he said with a laugh.

Ungerleider holds masses early in the evenings because on Sunday colonia residents must work, going out to the beach to sell whatever they can. He refuses to take up a collection during Mass. "I don't want any money in the church," he said. Instead, parishioners fill a basket with rice, beans, and the like. These sustain four families in need for a week, who help out around the church.

The day after the inauguration, I stood with the boyish-looking blue-eyed priest beneath the hot sun beside a section of the library still under construction. It was hard to fathom how he managed to do so much—and stay sane. A secret mantra? A medicinal tonic? I had to know. I asked him, how do you balance action and contemplation?

We were momentarily interrupted. He dashed off to explain to someone something about cisterns beneath the library and compressors for the air conditioning. Earlier he'd waxed enthusiastically about elevators. (He ended up ordering one from France because it was better made and cheaper—"globalization in action," he said.)

Action and contemplation? He told me that people often asked his mother how she remained calm with so many children. "If it doesn't draw blood, I don't worry about it," was her response, Ungerleider said.

Ungerleider downplays his gifts for founding institutions. At best he is the dreamer. It's the people who offer the know-how, and the donations—from large in size to "the widow's mite." "When people have a chance to follow up on an idea, they'll do it," he said.

Especially here, said author Luis Urrea, originally from Tijuana. "The border is a place of possibilities," he said with a smile. ■

2004

When in Doubt

Your pen is a gavel, calling the world to order.

People come forth with their testimonies. At a book fair in Houston an old man looks at you through smudged glasses and says, please write that people in mental hospitals aren't getting the right medicines because there are no Spanish speakers there to translate for them. At a senior center a woman says, write down that romero, rosemary, boiled in water and used as a rinse keeps hair thick and healthy. Another says, my mother used to sweep an egg over our bodies and pray to get rid of fevers. Write it down, because the young people don't know.

In the quiet of your room, you record the testimonies. You light a candle for Paloma Escobar Ledezma of Júarez. She disappeared, like hundreds of women workers there. Disappeared. The police did nothing. Twenty-seven days after she went missing, her body was found on the outskirts of the city. Women around the world hold demonstrations and demand action on behalf of the disappeared women of Júarez.

Too many times you walk away from the page to pour tea. But voices call you back: Grandpa Luis, author of corridos that were put to music, corridos about the beauty of New Mexico, a soldier fighting in the Philippines, an unjustly accused man, and civil rights champion Senator Dennis Chávez. Your great-grandmother Juanita, who wrote and read letters, in Spanish and English, for people in her village of Los Lunas south of Albuquerque, calls to you too. And you hear the voice of Grandma Lucy, whose students had nothing to write with. She cut wrapping paper she bought at Woolworth's and sewed it into tablets. She bought pencils, cut them in half, sharpened them, then gave them away.

In the quiet of your room, in the clatter of coffee shops, at the antiwar demonstration with your reporter's notebook—in all these places and more, remember that you are the daughter of Aztec scribes, known as the keepers of the red and black ink. Those colors flow from your pen.

You write even when you are not writing. Fall asleep with your notebook, and ink leaks into the page. A day or decade later you recognize the glyph on the paper and, with a great "aha," you set out to translate it into a poem. (Years of stained fingers: The ink is working its way to your heart. You will die writing.)

You write because you are so human. You fall in love the year that glaciers, for the first time in recorded history, melt and crack. You write a love poem.

A long time ago you wrote: "Because we have no word for light/We live in shadows." Still, you persist in the hunt for that word. You search for more paper as the candle honoring the spirit of Paloma Escobar Ledezma burns furiously. You e-mail friends in San Francisco, Vietnam, El Salvador, Africa, and Ireland. They know shadows; there is no burden too heavy for them. Poets all, they promise to search for the word for light in their languages and histories.

They put pen to paper and call the world to order. ∎

2003

Columnas en Tiempos de Guerra

Hell No

Stick It Up

I must love this country very much. Only a fool in love would order five hundred bumper stickers with the words "No Tax Cuts For The Rich" and then give them away for free. Call me naïve, call me codependent. I still think we can save the republic from ruin, vote by vote, protest by protest, bumper sticker by bumper sticker.

"No Tax Cuts For The Rich" was a breakthrough. I'm the type who wakes up at night abuzz with ideas for letters to the editor, and clever messages for T-shirts, signs, buttons, and bumper stickers. I have seldom followed through—a disgrace, given what a fan I am of the First Amendment, which has been so good to me.

Fellow poets debated the wording of our mobile manifesto. No Bush Tax Breaks For The Wealthy. Tax Cuts Add Up To Deficits Forever. In the end, symmetry and economy of wording won out. Weighing in at six words, No Tax Cuts For The Rich, could be broken in two lines and read in traffic without causing a wreck.

To say what you mean in as few words as possible: Both poet and citizen protester alike must rise to the occasion. Think back upon all the demonstrations you've been part of. What catches the eye of the passing driver or news reporter is a message that cuts to the chase, a declaration both elegant and brief.

In this regard, the left did well prior to the invasion of Iraq. Signs I saw at marches in Santa Fe and Albuquerque included (besides No War on Iraq): Support the Troops, Bring Them Home. Who Would Jesus Bomb? Peace Is Patriotic. Regime Change Begins At Home. And, War Is So 20th Century.

People used fresh Magic Markers and sturdy materials—no small feat given the left's long history of pale markings on thin poster board twisting in the wind. This time around, many people had their signs professionally printed and mounted. Mercifully, the spirit didn't move anyone to bring posters that proclaimed Save the Whales and the like. The imminent nature of the crisis focused minds. We stayed on message at a crucial time.

So, if you drive up behind me, here's what you'll read: No Tax Cuts For The Rich. And, Dissent Is Patriotic. For good measure, I stuck an American flag inside the back window. When I save up a little money (no tax cut for me), I'm having another bumper sticker made to honor the man who thinks duct tape on our windows could protect us in a terrorist attack. It will read, Lame Duct President. ∎

2003

Bitter Sweets

It was a sunny January afternoon. That night I would be at the Albuquerque Peace and Justice Center for what had become standing-room-only gatherings to plan demonstrations against the pending U.S. invasion of Iraq. But this particular afternoon my mind was on other things. I took a pile of cookbooks into a chilly but gloriously sunny porch. I was looking for something to fix for dinner. I ended up writing a poem instead.

JUST DESERT
(date halvah recipe from Iraq)

Chop two cups of dates, mix
With one half cup of walnuts,
And one half cup of almonds
(All finely chopped).
Blend everything in a bowl
And by hand make a roll
On a board sprinkled
With icing sugar.
Halweh is an Arabic
Word for sweet.
Iraq is one of the
World's biggest
Exporters of dates,
Or was . . .
Man cannot live
By oil alone. ■

2004

Night

Following is a record of dreams I had after the March 2003 U.S. invasion of Baghdad. All seemed to telegraph a story about the war that was outside the official story, outside the spin.

First dream: George W. Bush is about to make a speech about the war. A Native American man rushes to the podium. He intends to "translate" (this was the word in the dream) Bush's message for the nation—but from the perspective of peoples devastated by genocide. Secret Servicemen take him away. It is understood that the White House has its own people to interpret its message for the masses; it will allow no other perspectives.

Second dream: The faculty of the summer writing program at the William Joiner Center for the Study of War and Social Consequences have come together. (William Joiner, an African American Vietnam veteran, died of causes related to Agent Orange). It's time for orientation. We are at a motel overlooking an ancient city. It is in ruins. A new faculty member has joined us. I ask her what she'll be teaching. She answers, "translation."

Third dream: I'm in New York City in a small used bookstore, looking for poetry. The owner directs me to what he calls the "education and society" section. He pulls from the shelf a volume of poetry by the thirteenth-century Muslim mystic Rumi (he was born in what is now Afghanistan). I open it up. Its pages are filled with symbols and script I don't understand. But I know I must have this book. I know that somehow a translation will be found.

Finally, I am in a Baghdad hotel with my young niece and two nephews. The place is palatial, magnificent, with domes and arches; water cascades from tiled fountains. Saddam Hussein, wearing a suit and tie, shows up in the waiting area. He approaches us. He seems relaxed. He is kind to the children. I'm appalled. I excuse myself and search for a phone. I want desperately to call a newspaper. The world must know that the man whose statue was pulled down in the heat of "victory" is still alive.

One year ago this week the United States invaded Iraq, inaugurating those terrible nights when it was always tomorrow in Baghdad and the city blazed before us on our television sets. Turning now to those dreams (and what are dreams but drawings on the caves of our spirit, manifestations of a particular moment in history), I pick up echoes of answers to the question that haunts me: What must poets do?

The Native American man: Translate White House spin into truth, with an eye to history as lived by those who were not the "victors."

The veteran William Joiner: Stand at the edge of the ruined city and testify that there is no war without social consequences. Translate the message into every language, every action.

The Rumi book: Poets cannot remain in the obscurity and safety of the poetry section. We have to be involved in "education and society" and work to bring forth the voices of those whose concerns go untranslated into the public realm.

As to Saddam Hussein? He will live on, reincarnating again and again, unless our nation overcomes its addiction to oil—and to the care and feeding of ruthless dictators we deem "friendly" to the United States.

PS: In another recent dream I see a thick wall with a hole in it the size of a kiss. I'm told the damage resulted from a "nuclear bullet" made of depleted uranium. Next, I see about a dozen people in a small office who have devoted their lives to ending this type of warfare. They know they have to put the genie back in the bottle— and that they can do it as long as they redesign the bottle. This task is somehow linked to spirituality. On the wall is a picture of Dorothy Day. A pacifist and anarchist, she founded the Catholic

Worker movement, which has soup kitchens around the country. The movement promotes works of mercy, including visiting prisoners and the sick, and political witness, such as protests against war.

I can imagine what Dorothy Day is telling us: Ground your quest for peace in spiritual practice and work for justice. Even the technological beasts we have created may prove powerless against the weapons of spirit. ▪

2003–2004

Infinity and Other Matters

Recently my five-year-old nephew, Benjamin, announced, "You know what? Infinity never ends." He smiled his goofy smile. "Where did you learn that?" I asked. "My daddy told me," he said. The boy is my godson. It was Good Friday. I saw a teaching moment. "Well guess what? Jesus never ends," I said. He looked at me, underwhelmed. "Jesus is *already* infinity," he replied emphatically, frustrated by my medieval notions.

I must say that Benjamin's theology has advanced considerably. Last year I was pushing him on a swing tied to a tree in his front yard when apropos of nothing, he proclaimed, "Jesus is strong. He can hold up sixty-four ships." He went on, nearly shouting. "His mother is even stronger. She can hold up one hundred ships. She can hold up the whole night shift!"

I suppose he was thinking about his parents, who were away on a cruise. Still, I'd like to think my godmothering has something to do with his turn of mind. Benjamin was three years old and his little brother, David, was one when I warned their parents that if they didn't get the boys baptized soon I would personally dunk them in dishwater and do it myself.

They called the church. On a glorious spring day Benjamin let out a loud giggle as the deacon poured cold water on his forehead. David fell silent, but at least he did not hold his breath, turn blue, and faint, which was his habit.

After Benjamin and I got clear on infinity, David began to scream bloody murder. I ran to the playroom. A cross he'd made at school had come unglued and landed on his foot. I would think this would shake the faith of the most resilient three-year-old.

But by Easter Sunday he seemed to have recovered. He gripped his basket full of chocolates. I asked him, "Now what happened to Jesus today?" He looked irritated; he wanted to hunt for eggs. He thought for a second then shouted, "Easter!" He took off running.

It is not easy being an aunt nowadays. I dread the day when the boys ask me why women can't be priests, and why so much killing happens in the name of God. I believe the answers to the two questions are interrelated. I just hate to be the one to break the bad news.

In the meantime, I try to respond to our times with creativity. The other day David was running his finger over the letters of a yard sign that read, "No War Against Iraq." He thought the *q* was an *o*. He wanted to know what the sign said. I offered my interpretation. "It says, 'Use your words.'" He is one proud little boy, now that he knows how to read signs.

My niece, Rachel, is six. At my urging her parents took her to "The Easter Different: Harmony and Peace," a program at the gallery of photographer Douglas Kent Hall called Space D, in Albuquerque. The program consisted of music by The Rebbe's Orkestra and poetry by Palestinian American poet Lisa Suhair Majaj.

Drummer Lynn Gottlieb, a rabbi and peace activist, opened the set of music with a statement. She said she takes to heart what her Palestinian friends have told her time and again. "Jesus was a Palestinian Jew living under occupation," Gottlieb said. The group went on to play Middle Eastern music, including an Iraqi melody. For an instant I believed peace was possible.

I looked over at Rachel. She was mesmerized, watching the musicians. Her eyes drifted upward to take in a photograph of Jimi Hendrix. Her cheeks were turning red as a beet. Before the program ended, her parents hustled her out and drove to urgent care to treat her hives. But she got to hear most of Majaj's work, including "A Few Reasons to Oppose the War."

"because our bodies are soft and easily harmed
and destruction is a way of dying, not living," read Majaj.

"because we are so utterly human
and so prone to grief . . .
"because each morning the wildflowers outside my window
raise their yellow faces to the sun
because we are all, each one of us,
in love with the light."   ■

2003

Hurts

My earliest memories are of the Vietnam War on a black-and-white television in the den at dinnertime: a naked Vietnamese girl on fire, U.S. soldiers coming home in body bags. I stood at the edges of the den, for years at the edges of history, a child whose father, a major in the Marine Corps reserves, could have been called up at any moment. I remember Walter Cronkite announcing the daily body counts, and because this knowledge hurt too much, I told myself a story: that my father, who was in his early thirties, was too old to be sent off to that war. I believed this story absolutely—except when the mail arrived. After school, if my parents were not around, I rifled through envelopes left on top of the piano, in search of a Washington, D.C., return address. If I found such a letter, I pressed it against the windowpane, up to the light, trying to make out the signature of President Lyndon B. Johnson. Surely he would write my father personally, I thought, if he were to take him from us, destroying my world. In wartime children don't think logically, they think apocalyptically.

When I was an adult, I asked my father about what really had been at stake. To my surprise he said that he had had his sea bag ready to go, with his dog tags and required changes of clothing. He had had his papers in order. It was no family secret, he said, that he could have been called up. But children are magicians when it comes to repressing knowledge that hurts too much. I remember nothing about the sea bag. I just remember feeling sick with fear when I saw the mail sitting on the piano, and relief whenever I told myself that my father was too old to go to Vietnam.

Now it's my turn to grieve for the children: of U.S. soldiers, of Iraq, all wise to the ways of war, wiser than our cowardly president who has banned pictures of coffins from appearing on television.

The warmongers sleep well. The children never do. ∎

2004

And to the Republic

United States flags were everywhere at the Christmas dances at Zia Pueblo in 2001, the year of the Twin Towers disaster: flags on hatbands, hunting rifles, bows and arrows, slung over shoulders, flopping from waistbands, sewn into shirts. One man had even painted his face red, white, and blue.

"God bless America. I pray for you America." The powerful chant swirled up with the drumming as the first of about twenty men made their way across the dirt plaza. Many were veterans wearing their military fatigues. Others had lost family members in wars. Love of country was no abstraction for them.

Another group, younger men and boys, appeared on the plaza wearing antlered headgear and white moccasins. The annual Buffalo Dance was beginning. The dancers leaned forward on short white sticks and became deer. At the center a young woman in traditional dress, and a man with the head of a buffalo, danced in a bitter cold wind, beneath a blazing sun.

Until that Christmas day, I had forgotten how much I loved the flag. I loved it the first time I saw students burn it in protest during the Vietnam War. They happened to be outside my grandmother's house, a few blocks from the University of New Mexico, on the corner of Silver and Gold Southeast.

I was perhaps ten years old at the time. Yet I sensed what an awesome thing the flag was, so invested with meaning, with great purpose, that the burning of it amounted to a kind of sacrifice. The republic for which it stood must have engaged in actions so terrible as to be almost beyond words. The flag in flames was a cry from the gut, a prayer.

As of mid-February 2004 nearly 550 U.S. soldiers have died in Iraq. Among these: Lori Piestewa of the Hopi Nation, the first known Native American female soldier to die fighting in combat on foreign soil. I will not burn a flag to protest this war. It is enough to remember Lori, and to honor her with prayers for an end to war everywhere. ▪

2004

Hell No

Teenagers who think they might seek conscientious objector status if the draft is revived need to start documenting their beliefs now, said Albuquerque attorney Tova Indritz. The draft is designed for swift implementation, said Indritz, leaving precious little time for a young man to gather evidence of his beliefs to present to a draft board.

Indritz has spoken to groups of young people about this issue. "Many people don't realize that the entire mechanism and apparatus for implementing the draft is in place—the Selective Service board, and all the local draft boards, and the appeal boards.

"And according to the Selective Service, they've even prepared two drums to be ready for a lottery at a moment's notice, one with the numbers 1 through 365, and one with all the birth dates of the year," she said.

She laid out what she said would be a likely scenario should the president call for a draft in the name of a "national emergency."

"On Day 1, Congress passes a law" to reinstate the draft, and the president signs the bill the same day or the next, said Indritz. A lottery, "which could take as few as two hours," is held the next day, she said, to match each birth date with a number 1 through 365.

The Selective Service then immediately issues letters to those men who turn twenty years old in that calendar year whose numbers matching their birthdays were drawn in the lottery. The letters contain orders to appear for a "physical, mental, and moral evaluation" ten days from the postmarked date of the letter, said Indritz, citing government documents.

Indritz explained that a claim for conscientious objector status must be turned in before the date of the evaluation. A draft board then schedules a hearing. If the board turns down the request, and if subsequent appeals fail, a new date is set for a young man to proceed with his evaluation.

"It can't be that you pass the physical," said Indritz, "then start thinking about conscientious objector status."

According to the law, a conscientious objector is one who is "opposed to war in any form," Indritz said. "You can't be against the Vietnam War and for World War II," she said.

One's views must be grounded in a "moral belief," a "religion or something equivalent to a religion in your life," said Indritz. One need not believe in God, nor reject the idea of personal self-defense, she said.

Before appearing before the draft board, a written statement should be prepared explaining how one arrived at one's beliefs and how those beliefs have influenced how one lives one's life, Indritz explained.

What kind of supporting evidence might one submit to a draft board? Indritz said evidence can include letters of reference from teachers and religious leaders, or their actual appearance as witnesses; journal entries regarding one's attitudes to war (these might include responses to sermons, speakers, or a relative's participation in earlier wars); proof of participation in antiwar protests; reading lists and proof of subscriptions to religious or political publications that oppose war.

"If you have evidence from the week before, that's not going to be as good as something you've kept from age fourteen," said Indritz.

A man can also start to build his case the day he registers with Selective Service. Indritz said that the registrant can write in the margins of the form, "I am a conscientious objector." He should then make several copies and mail one to himself on the same day he mails the official form. After he receives his copy, he should save the copy and the postmarked envelope.

Registering with Selective Service is required by law. It must be done within thirty days of a young man's eighteenth birthday.

Failure to do so is punishable by up to five years in prison and $250,000 in fines. No one, however, has been prosecuted since the 1980s, Indritz said.

But there are "other prices" that people pay, she explained. Failing to register makes one ineligible for federal student aid and federal jobs for life. Numerous states also have penalties. Arizona, for example, denies state employment to those who fail to register; Arkansas denies driver's licenses.

Technically, a man can submit his registration as late as his twenty-sixth birthday; though he still risks prosecution, the government is obligated to accept the form. But failure to register by age twenty-six means that "one can never, ever" get certain types of government jobs, said Indritz. These are consequences that young people rarely think through, she said.

A new draft is not a far-fetched scenario, according to Brian Cross, development director for the Central Committee for Conscientious Objectors. Cross told me in an interview that the organization has been besieged by phone calls since the September 11, 2001, terrorist attacks. Callers seeking information have included people inside and outside the military, including concerned parents. The committee, which has offices in Oakland and Philadelphia, was founded after World War II.

"For every request for literature we received in August 2001, we received four hundred requests in October 2001," said Cross. The organization's GI Rights Hotline received about 2,100 calls last year, and Cross expects to log more calls this year. The hot line provides information about objector exemptions as well as all other legitimate bases for a discharge.

Cross's work includes educating religious groups about what they can do to support conscientious objectors. He cited as an example Quakers who include in their minutes of a meeting that "Harry Smith has decided to become a conscientious objector," notes that can be used as documentation before a draft board.

Cross said that outreach to Catholics has become a top priority for him. Churches need to know how they can be responsive to conscientious objectors, he said, by providing information and support. "We want to help Catholic churches gear up to become centers for peace," said Cross. ∎

2003

Terrorist Times

Marcus Page of Gallup, New Mexico, is a committed pacifist with deep roots in the Catholic Worker movement. He hosts a radio talk show called *Cultivating Peace* and has produced a radio documentary about Catholic anarchist Ammon Hennacy. The thirty-six-year-old radio rebel, who wears his hair in a Mohawk, also works with community-oriented micropower stations, sometimes known as free or "pirate" radio. Page is also affiliated with a number of peace groups. Among these are the Nevada Desert Experience and the Global Network Against Weapons and Nuclear Power in Space.

In May 2001 Page participated in a prayer action at Vandenberg Air Force Base near Santa Barbara, California. The largest space command facility in the United States, Vandenberg is best known for its national missile defense tests in promotion of Star Wars. Page described the action, which was coordinated with the Los Angeles Catholic Worker affinity group, as "a prayer to sanctify the land and to stop the violence." He was subsequently found guilty of trespassing and is serving a year's probation.

Page recently drove to Tucson with two friends to check out our local peace fair. His pleasant visit took a bizarre turn, however, en route back to New Mexico. He called me after returning to Gallup to tell me what happened.

A police officer near Mammoth, Arizona, Page said, stopped the group for allegedly speeding. Page, who was driving his friend's car, concedes he might have been going five miles over the speed limit. He gave the officer his social security number, which was relayed to a dispatcher. But Page was not merely ticketed. The cop proceeded to handcuff him, justifying the action with the claim that Page was "affiliated with a terrorist organization."

Page thought he was joking until a backup car and a canine unit showed up. Not wanting to provoke the cop, Page did not inquire about the "terrorist organization." Instead, he made small talk with one of the cops.

"During our wait for the police to search everything, one cop stayed with us and told us all about Jesus Christ the Savior in response to our comments on Christian pacifism," said Page. "The Christian cop claimed that God ordains some governments to use violence, including the USA."

Thankfully, the group was let go within about an hour.

"I'm not one to ever admit being angry . . . but it did cause stress," said Page.

Given our nation's dark history of repressing dissent, one must wonder what activists of all stripes will confront as President George W. Bush escalates his antiterrorist rhetoric.

Bush's problem is that he is waging war not on specific criminals but with "evil" in general. And demonology makes for irrational military policy. In Bush's worldview, dissenters are soft on evil-doers and should be dealt with by curtailing their civil rights.

Meanwhile, Page, a gentle spirit, is willing to give the cop the benefit of the doubt. The guy was "fumbling, decent, not nasty," said Page, who wondered if he had confused the concept of an activist group with a terrorist group. In our post–9/11 world, I fear such confusion will become epidemic. ▪

2001

Tongues

When the United States invaded Iraq, the word "translation" appeared in a number of my dreams. I suppose it should come as no surprise. As a Chicana I am the daughter of Malintzin, the mother of the mestizo people. Fluent in several Native tongues, she learned Spanish when the conquistadores arrived in the New World. She acted as translator for Hernan Cortéz. She gave birth to his child, the first Mexican, a child of Indian and European ancestry. The old story is that she betrayed the Indian people, fell in love with Cortéz, and told him what he needed to know about the Aztecs so that he could carry out the conquest.

Feminist scholars have offered other possible versions of the story. Love? She was property. And useful because of her facility with languages. I can easily imagine her using her position with Cortéz to try to undermine him. Maybe she tried to invent ways to throw Cortéz and his men off track: lying to him or passing clues about his plans to the Indians. The Native peoples believed Cortéz was the pale god on a horse who'd come across the waters as predicted in their prophecies. Maybe Malintzin tried to say to them *no, he is just a man.*

It's also possible that Malintzin perceived the conquest as inevitable, especially given the alliances Cortéz built with Native groups who had themselves been conquered by the Aztecs. Perhaps she hoped her words could lead to some sort of peaceful coexistence among Indians and the conquerors. Was she a traitor? A failure? Do these words even apply in the face of an apocalypse that was impossible to prevent?

The scenario that tugs at me the most is this one: I imagine she tried to thwart a holocaust by translating not just the Indian's words, but also their worldviews, their stories. But she miscalculated. The Spaniards may have listened to what the Indians said, but they dared not hear what was meant. To wrestle with what another person means, and not just says, is risky business. The speaker might become human to the listener. Ultimately, the Indians could exist only insofar as they remained in the shadow of the Christian cross and the Spanish crown.

Amadou Diallo, a Haitian-born man, was living and working in New York when in 2000 he was shot forty-one times while he reached for his wallet as police cornered him in their search for another man. Not long after that horror, which riveted the nation, I had a dream in which I was on a small island. Overhead helicopter gun ships took aim at dark-skinned people, young and old. In terror they huddled against the bluffs. I shouted against the wind, at the helicopters: "No, stop, they have histories!" But as I woke up I knew it was too late. A massacre had ensued.

Just as the men in the helicopters saw nonhumans, the Spaniards saw savages. They could not see or hear people with histories: those stories told over time, be they origin tales, remedies, prayers, parables, humor, or accounts of victories and defeats.

And this is what nations and individuals do, still. None of us is exempt. We flatten people, assume they have no stories, and in doing so inflict a thousand psychic injuries upon one another. Or we simply bomb whole nations.

Poets everywhere share the struggle of Malintzin: We must translate not only one another's works, but one another's lives. ∎

2004

Home on the Range

The day before Easter Sunday we decided to go to Open House at Trinity Site, New Mexico, where the first atom bomb, on July 16, 1945, splintered the sky. Late Friday, my friends and I took off from Tucson, driving seven hours to Alamagordo, New Mexico, where we called it quits for the night. Alamagordo is eighty-five miles southeast of Trinity Site. It is a small town boasting a "Jesus Christ Is Lord Over Alamagordo" billboard. People here are, as they used to say, kindly. It's the sort of place where you can still talk a motel manager into letting a few extra people crash in a room at little extra charge.

It was late by the time we got checked in. We had to rise early to drive out to the site; I doubted we would get much sleep. I offered to spring for a bottle of wine. Two of our group made a run to a twenty-four-hour Wal-Mart. They returned with wine, plastic goblets, white bread, and peanut butter.

But by then I had put on my pajamas and retreated into my shell, a true Cancerian indulging in a melancholy that dazzles the gullible who mistake our blank stares for deep thoughts.

My Generation X friends tuned in to a television show teeming with obscure references; they laughed knowingly. I drank down my wine, closed my eyes, and considered man's capacity for evil. I tried to picture the parcel of land known as Ground Zero. Having come all this way, I wanted nothing less than to see the devil himself, red fork flashing. I would leave Trinity Site in a blaze of goose bumps and insights and fresh metaphors for global catastrophe. At the very least, Open House would improve my writing.

Early the next morning hundreds of people queued up in cars at Alamagordo's shopping mall. Smiling volunteers orchestrated traffic like school crossing guards. They passed out free booklets called *Trinity Site, 1945–1995,* a cheery history of the bomb. I began reading aloud from the booklet as we rolled away from the parking lot.

"In deciding whether to visit Ground Zero at Trinity Site, the following information may prove helpful," I read.

"Radiation levels in the fenced, Ground Zero area are low. On an average [sic] the levels are only 10 times greater than the region's natural background radiation. A one-hour visit to the inner fenced area will result in a whole body exposure of one-half to one milliroentgen (mrem).

"To put this in perspective . . . the Department of Energy says we receive between 35 and 50 milliroentgens every year from the sun and from 20 to 35 milliroentgens every year from our food. Living in a brick house adds 50 milliroentgens of exposure every year compared to living in a frame house."

I did a little mrem math in my head. Relax, I told my friends. It's not Ground Zero we must fear but all the rest of life. Rocks, soil, air, water, food, X-rays, watch dials and smoke detectors—virtually everything, including "cosmic rays from space," is emanating mrems night and day, the booklet explained.

I read on. Trinity Site was looking better all the time.

But then came the disclaimer, the bold-lettered spin you find on everything from microwave ovens to condom packages.

"Although radiation levels are low, some feel any extra exposure should be avoided. The decision is yours. It should be noted that small children and pregnant women are potentially more at risk than the rest of the population and are generally considered groups who should only receive exposure in conjunction with medical diagnosis and treatment. Again, the choice is yours."

I handed the booklet over to the next reader. The landscape turned dusty. The car rocked me to sleep.

When I woke up I was sure we had taken a wrong turn, ending up at a carnival. Outside the Ground Zero gates tourists swarmed to souvenir booths, food carts, and portable outdoor restrooms. Military police chatted with families setting out paper plates on picnic tables. Food vendors flipped hamburgers on open grills in a swirl of smoke. A vegetarian (except when I eat meat), I would have bought a burger, but the line was too long.

My friend asked to take my picture. Others were doing the same. They posed in front of steel bones poking up out of the ground: all that remains of the one-hundred-foot tower upon which the bomb ticked toward its destiny, 5:29:45 A.M. Mountain War Time, after an hour-and-a-half delay due to bad weather.

I stood before the remains of a 214-ton steel jug named Jumbo. It was to have served as a container for the bomb, but the chain reaction failed to materialize according to the scientists' plans. By 1946 the giant thermos had outlived its usefulness. The army detonated eight 500-pound bombs inside Jumbo, blowing off each end. A dashing blue sky poured through Jumbo's gaping mouth. I thought of Stonehenge. I smiled for the camera.

We walked around. It was a beautiful day. Photographs documenting the history of the bomb were posted on the chain link fence inside Ground Zero like Stations of the Cross. We moved from picture to picture in a trance. The words "mushroom cloud" did justice to the explosion's lush appearance.

On my way back to the gate, I searched the ground for trinitite. The glassy green particles came into being when the heat of the bomb congealed steel and desert sand. The fragments are like something you would buy at a bead show to make jewelry out of. Except that they are radioactive. Officials warned tourists not to remove the trinitite. I tossed the strange gems back on the ground.

But weeks later I'm wondering why I didn't slip some trinitite into my jeans pocket and walk out: away from the Fatman bomb casing and information booth, the stands cluttered with mugs, visors, key rings, hat pins, T-shirts—memorabilia from which the mushroom cloud was conspicuously absent.

A glittering speck of trinitite? The risk has less to do with radioactivity than human memory and its short half-life. In all likelihood I would show off my trinket, then set it aside in the same way the U.S. government sets aside a day for Open House at Ground Zero. Instead of asking history's hard questions about war, I would do everything in my power to avoid them. ▪

1996

October

The ash tree in my front yard—with its vaulted branches and massive trunk—is close to fifty years old. I've lived in this house only two years; still, the tree is like an old friend. The tree's many dead branches moved my father to consult an arborist. We learned that the tree was diseased and had, perhaps, five years left.

I tried to disregard the news, but it worked its way into my marrow as surely as pests had burrowed into the branches above my head. Days after receiving the prognosis, I burst into tears. I remembered, as if it had happened yesterday, the removal of a dead peach tree I so loved in childhood, how I looked at it one last time out my bedroom window, then turned and blocked my ears against the howl of the chainsaw.

My grief for our fragile environment often erupts in very personal terms, but its roots are political. Everywhere trees are being felled at an alarming rate, contributing among other things to global warming, a fact the Republican administration has been loath to confront. The forests and other lands that bring us joy, sustenance, and meaning—the places that form the setting of our ancestral stories—are disappearing, and we humans may well be an endangered species as a result.

I decided to talk with the arborist myself. Could we do anything to improve the quality of the tree's remaining years? He suggested dead-wooding it, removing the almost one-third of branches that showed no signs of life.

I tried not to lash out. "That sounds like a mastectomy," I said. "You don't do that for cosmetic reasons." He patiently went over the benefits of dead-wooding, which included helping rid the tree of pests that could harm the robust branches. He also recommended complementary therapies such as deep root feeding. His answers satisfied me. I'd already called another arborist for a second opinion, and he had said much the same thing.

"Have at it," I said. "But for God's sake be careful. Try to leave as much of its original shape as possible." To escape the wail of the chainsaw, I took off to a nearby café with my laptop and consoled myself with the thought that my tree was getting a "haircut." We all need a new look, I thought.

I was pleasantly surprised when I got up the nerve to come home. Where once dead branches cluttered the sky, a brilliant blue shone through. The thriving branches looked greener than before. The arborist found a bat hanging on a dead branch. We let it be.

The next day I turned on the radio—then, to make sure I wasn't imagining things, turned it up full volume.

The 2004 Nobel Peace Prize, said Amy Goodman of *Democracy Now,* had been awarded to an African woman, Wangari Maathai. Founder of the Green Belt movement, Maathai has for thirty years mobilized poor women to plant some 30 million trees in her native Kenya. The movement has also educated people about the values of indigenous food crops and trained them in methods of organic farming.

I went on the Internet. "Peace on earth depends on our ability to secure our living environment," said the Nobel committee in its statement about Maathai. "She has taken a holistic approach to sustainable development that embraces democracy, human rights, and women's rights in particular. She thinks globally and acts locally."

Peace on earth. The dream will be realized not only by putting down arms but by putting down roots—and standing up to governments, as has Maathai, that would repress movements toward environmental justice. Like Eve, we need to befriend trees. We must eat of the fruit of knowledge that will guide us toward Eden—before the powers that be wipe the memory of forests from our collective consciousness for good. ■

2004

Confesiones de una Chicana Berlitz
A Spanish Translation

Note: Following is the title essay, "Confessions of a Berlitz-Tape Chicana," translated into Spanish by Héctor Contreras López of Chihuahua. I offer it here to my hermanos and hermanas on the other side, el otro lado. I first read this essay, in translation, in Tijuana, on a panel with other Chicano writers and activists.

While there, we made a visit to a section of the border wall that meanders off into the depths of the Pacific Ocean. On the other side, border patrol officers waited and watched. On our side, a family gathered near what appeared to be an opening in the wall. It was hard to tell; the fog was thick. For a few minutes I thought I heard La Llorona weeping for those who had drowned in the brutal waves in hopeless attempts to swim around the wall to the United States.

I walked up to the wall and began to pick at it like a scab, and came away with a piece smaller than my palm, a rusty relic that now sits beside my computer. I believe it's possible, piece by piece, word by word, to dismember that wall, and remember, at last, who we are. One people. For now, this translated essay is the note I am slipping through the gash before the fog lifts.

Estamos en todas partes y ya es hora de salir del clóset. Me refiero a la generación que, al menos en parte, ha vivido en el silencio, a aquellos que compramos libros con títulos como *Aprenda español en diez minutos mientras toma la siesta.* Somos los chicanos que estudiamos con casets en nuestros autos y en el trayecto al trabajo murmuramos frases para dirigir a un taxista argentino hacia el hotel o para ordenar tapas en un bar en España.

En casa, hojeamos catálogos de clases en el extranjero; imaginamos que adquirimos el español como podríamos adquirir un guardarropa. Pero todo cuesta: la colegiatura para las escuelas de idiomas, los boletos para Guatemala y un par de sandalias a la moda. Sale caro estar entre los turistas de la lengua a los que mi padre llama "Sandalistas."

Sin embargo, qué atractivo suena. ¡Inmersión total! ¡En un país extranjero! Al menos según el testimonio de algunos de nuestros amigos, mucho después de haber olvidado la mayor parte de lo que aprendieron.

Pero nosotros sabemos que las cosas no son así. Después de todo, vivimos en una región ocupada de México e incluso más allá, en cada barrio y en cada suburbio donde habitan los latinos. Llegamos con ensalada de papa y tamales a ruidosas reuniones familiares que hacen que en los funerales incluso las lágrimas valgan la pena. Ahí nos encontramos a tías con nombres como Consuelo, Elvira o Maudi, y a tíos Bamba, Elfigo y Juan. Después de la comida se dejan caer en los sillones de la sala y comen pastel en platos desechables; hablan un español espeso y dulce, veteado de inglés. ¿Inmersión total? Nada mejor que la familia.

Mientras tanto, los primos nos juntamos y renovamos los votos para mejorar nuestro español. Crecimos escuchando el idioma—usualmente en las cocinas de los familiares—, pero en la mayoría de los casos contestábamos en inglés. Nos referimos a nuestro español "mocho" como si fuera un hueso fracturado y hablamos de cómo, cuando menos lo esperamos, el idioma "regresa," como si siempre hubiera estado ahí.

Nos avergonzamos, pues algo precioso se desmoronó ante nuestros ojos. Y somos persistentes; queremos que nuestros hijos adquieran la fluidez por la que nosotros todavía estamos luchando. Después del nacimiento de mi sobrina Rachel, recé el Padre Nuestro en varias ocasiones con ella en mis brazos: Danos hoy el pan de cada día. Desde el primer día quería empezar a abrir sus vías neuronales no sólo hacia a Dios, también hacia el español.

Mi propia educación en español comenzó durante mi primer año de vida, cuando mi padre fue enviado a Okinawa. Mi madre y yo vivimos con mis abuelos maternos, quienes diariamente cruzaban la frontera entre el español y el inglés, hablando sobre política y el póker. Tiempo después, mis abuelos me llevaron a la Primera Iglesia de las Asambleas de Dios, donde Dios daba a conocer su gloria no sólo en lenguas, también en español, por medio de la voz de un predicador que, señalando hacia la Biblia, gritaba y lloraba. Entonces, mis oídos se abrieron. En los días subsiguientes, a la hora de la cena, solía acurrucarme junto con mi prima a la orilla de las conversaciones de los adultos: sabíamos lo que ellos estaban diciendo cuando cambiaban al español para hablar de sus cosas.

En casa, hablando por teléfono, mi papá iba fácilmente del español al inglés y viceversa, variando sus inflexiones dependiendo si se trataba de un anciano del norte de Nuevo México o de algún viejo camarada del barrio. No recuerdo que mi mamá haya hablado mucho en español; introvertida, abrumada tal vez por los talentos de mi padre, el español residía menos en su lengua que en su oído.

Con pocas excepciones, los niños de la colonia y en la escuela primaria hablaban inglés; lo mismo sucedía con los niños en la televisión, como en *Perdidos en el espacio* o *La familia Partridge*. Sin embargo, el quinto año escolar trajo una sorpresa: una niña de Puerto Rico llegó a nuestra clase y nos hicimos amigas. Yo ejercité mi español, ella su inglés; ambas fortalecimos nuestros músculos lingüísticos hasta que, un día, a ella la cambiaron de escuela.

Ese mismo año escribí un trabajo y usé una palabra que, según mi maestro, no existía. Siempre había recibido buenas calificaciones en mis trabajos escritos; los maestros decían que mi comprensión del inglés era avanzada para mi edad, gracias en gran parte, creo, a que mi madre me llevaba más seguido a la biblioteca que a la iglesia. Le señalé la palabra en el diccionario y el maestro la aceptó. El incidente aún me parece importante, lo recuerdo todavía muy vívidamente. Esa oscura palabra del inglés, tan oscura que no puedo recordarla, fue no sólo una palabra, sino una vía: el dominio del inglés junto con su lado oscuro, el control de las personas. En aquel momento, todo lo que sentí fue la emoción de haber "descubierto" una palabra. Tuvieron que pasar varios años antes de que pudiera comprender la política de las lenguas en las cuales nos comunicamos y presenciara el privilegio que tienen los que pueden esgrimir el inglés como una espada.

Durante los fines de semana, pasaba las noches con mi abuela materna. Ella solía pararse cuan alta era y ordenar, no pedir, a mi padre: "Déjala, déjala"—refiriéndose a mí—, déjala comerse ese dulce, quedarse otra noche, brincar en la cama. En silencio, mi papá se encogía de hombros. Mi abuela me había hechizado con una palabra en español que significaba amor incondicional.

Mi padre fue elegido para formar parte del Consejo Municipal de las Escuelas de Albuquerque en 1969; él fue el primer chicano en ocupar ese puesto, lo cual sucedió inmediatamente después de un acontecimiento memorable: la aprobación del Acta Bilingüe de 1967. Mi padre participó en los grandes debates de la época, debates que aún no terminan. Un bando veía el uso del español como un mero escalón para aprender inglés; el bando al que mi padre pertenecía imaginaba el salón de clases como un lugar donde los niños podrían adquirir fluidez en los dos idiomas.

Mi papá me insistió para que tomara español cuando estaba en la secundaria y en la preparatoria. Yo sobresalí en mis clases. "Tu acento es perfecto," decían mis maestros. En la universidad me esforcé aún más y me inscribí en una clase de nivel avanzado. Después de graduarme, me puse a leer cada mañana a los grandes poetas hispanoamericanos, desde Gabriela Mistral hasta César Vallejo, en la vieja plaza del centro de Albuquerque, durante largos momentos de éxtasis. Me detenía a escuchar los chismes de las *viejitas* que salían de misa de 7:00 de la iglesia de San Felipe; me moría por preguntarles cuánto tiempo habían vivido cerca de esa plaza del siglo XVIII y qué tanto había cambiado la vida. Pero la marea del inglés hablado era demasiado fuerte; para cuando había traducido en mi mente lo que quería decir, ellas ya se habían ido. Con el tiempo, sin embargo, ese deseo ha seguido creciendo dentro de mí. Puedo conversar en español por períodos más y más largos, olvidando que "no tengo fluidez" (lo cual podría ser una definición de fluidez).

Una tarde, me encontré en un naranjal en las afueras de Phoenix, donde muchos refugiados guatemaltecos vivían bajo los árboles, tratando de encontrar un coyote que los llevara a Florida. Las iglesias traían la comida mientras una clínica móvil se instalaba y un grupo de mujeres exhaustas se formaba en una fila. Una enfermera me dio una carpeta: "Andamos cortos de personal—me dijo—, ¿podrías encargarte del registro?" Mis pulmones se llenaron como velas. Les pregunté a las mujeres cuándo habían tenido su última regla; les pregunté sobre su viaje. Mi lengua se había liberado.

Otra escena me viene a la mente: voy caminando por el campus de la Universidad de Harvard con un poeta vietnamita. "Beautiful night"—es casi lo único que podemos decirnos antes de caer en el silencio. De repente, él se voltea hacia mí y me pregunta, en español, si hablo español. "Sí—le contesto—; ¿dónde lo aprendiste tú?" "En Cuba"—me dice. Hablamos sin parar. Nuestras palabras son como las piezas del rompecabezas de un niño que vamos armando para trazar un mapa de nuestras vidas.

En el 2001, el novelista salvadoreño Manlio Argueta me invitó a su país a una conferencia de literatura testimonial de la posguerra civil; me pidió que hablara sobre mi novela *Lengua madre,* que cuenta la historia de un refugiado salvadoreño y su amante chicana. La historia se desarrolla durante el Movimiento Santuario de los años ochenta, cuando muchos ciudadanos norteamericanos desafiaron las leyes de inmigración y abrieron las puertas de sus casas a refugiados guatemaltecos y salvadoreños.

Escribí mi presentación en español, sin problema. El legado de nuestra generación se manifiesta en que lo que no ha sido dicho, con frecuencia se apresura, con una extraña facilidad, a nuestras manos y luego a la página. Aquellos años de ejercicios de escritura en clase seguramente habían ayudado. Sin embargo, como en los naranjales en las afueras de Phoenix y en el campus de la Universidad de Harvard, un ansia por comunicarme me dejaba trastabillando alegremente, tratando de encontrar la palabra precisa o por lo menos una aproximación. Esa ansia corta a lo largo del miedo a esa palabra que no llega a ser la palabra precisa, a lo largo del miedo a la imperfección. Y también a lo largo de la culpa y de la vergüenza.

La culpa se manifiesta cuando nos decimos: "Soy latino, debería hablar bien español." La vergüenza le sigue cuando estamos con los que hablan con fluidez y nos da miedo hablar. Estas emociones son tan fuertes que no sirve de mucho saber que una gran cantidad de cosas en nuestra historia han conspirado contra esa fluidez; el movimiento *English Only* es sólo una de sus manifestaciones más virulentas. ¿Quién no ha escuchado una historia (recordada por alguno de los mayores o incluso por uno de nuestros contemporáneos) de castigos impuestos por hablar español en la escuela, desde bocas lavadas con jabón hasta la ubicación en clases para niños con problemas de aprendizaje?

Y algunos de los nuestros son nuestros peores enemigos: los intelectuales y activistas con actitudes de soy-más-chicano o más-mexicano-que-tú, que nos miran por encima del hombro, quizá porque reflejamos tan explícitamente su lucha para encontrar su propia voz.

En una ocasión me tocó participar en un panel con el poeta puertorriqueño Martín Espada y con Claribel Alegría, de El Salvador. Una mujer del público se puso de pie y nos acusó: "¿Cómo se atreven a hablar como latinos, sobre la literatura de los latinos, en inglés?"

Desde hace tiempo he mantenido que el español es una lengua paterna, la de los conquistadores. Nuestras verdaderas lenguas maternas son las lenguas indígenas, muchas de ellas borradas del mapa durante el genocidio. Sueño con un día cuando nosotros los latinos seamos trilingües, o por lo menos estudiemos una tercera lengua: quechua, tewa, yoheme, diné, náhuatl; los caminos hacia la recuperación son innumerables. Como respuesta a la mujer, logré comunicar algo así, incluso mientras sentía que una espada había sido esgrimida hacia mi garganta.

Una de las protagonistas de *Lengua madre* es Soledad, madrina de María, quien es amante de José Luis, que llega a Estados Unidos de El Salvador. Soledad pasa de contrabando refugiados centroamericanos y le da toda clase de consejos a María, desde la vida fuera de la ley hasta los remedios caseros. Cuando se da cuenta de la relación amorosa entre María y José Luis, le aconseja a su ahijada en una carta: "Mijita, si vas a perder la cabeza por este muchacho, por lo menos ponte lista y usa tu experiencia para apuntalar tu español, ¿cómo crees que yo aprendí inglés? ¿Recuerdas a aquel bueno para nada mi primer marido del que te hablé alguna vez? Bueno, éramos jóvenes y estábamos enamorados y lo que él decía cuando estábamos juntos no necesitaba traducción. Uno desarrolla un tercer oído cuando se enamora de un hombre que habla otra lengua. Primero, batallas para entender lo que dice; luego, empiezas a escuchar lo que en realidad está diciendo; y al final, la relación se termina. Pero tú eres lo mejor de todo." Soledad termina la carta diciéndole: "Escribe pronto, en español. Si no sabes una palabra, invéntala."

Arrastrada por la música del español, mi generación desarrolló un tercer oído; nos enamoramos de lo que oíamos, y ese amor nos ha sacado de nuestra soledad. "Quiero redescubrir el secreto del gran discurso y del gran incendio," escribe Aimé Césaire en su *Cuaderno de retorno al país natal*. "Quiero decir tormenta. Quiero decir río." Nosotros, los que hemos luchado para encontrar nuestra voz, tenemos el secreto del gran discurso y del gran incendio. *Tempestad, río*; palabra por palabra, estamos regresando a casa. ∎

Traducción: Héctor Contreras López, 2003